SETTING THE RECORD STRAIGHT

Capturing the Voices of Women in Welsh Politics 1999–2021

EDITED BY CATRIN EDWARDS
AND KATE SULLIVAN

First published in Great Britain in 2024 by Honno Press
D41 Hugh Owen Building, Penglais Campus, Aberystwyth University,
Aberystwyth, Ceredigion, SY23 3DY

www.honno.co.uk

A catalogue record for this book is available from the British Library.
Published with the financial support of the Books Council of Wales.

ISBN: 978-1-91290-572-0
Ebook ISBN: 978-1-91290-573-7

Typesetting and design: Tanwen Haf/Books Council of Wales
Printed by: 4Edge

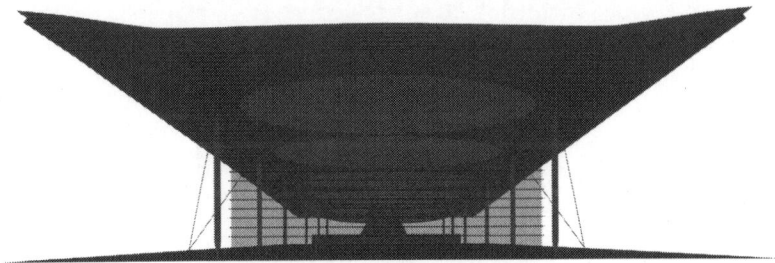

SETTING THE RECORD STRAIGHT

Capturing the Voices of Women in Welsh Politics 1999–2021

EDITED BY CATRIN EDWARDS
AND KATE SULLIVAN

h

honno

CONTENTS

CONTRIBUTORS

Hannah Blythyn

Dawn Bowden

Michelle Brown

Jayne Bryant

Eleanor Burnham

Angela Burns

Christine Chapman

Jane Davidson

Janet Davies

Jocelyn Davies

Suzy Davies

Tamsin Dunwoody

Sue Essex

Delyth Evans

Nerys Evans

Lisa Francis

Veronica German

Janice Gregory

Lesley Griffiths

Siân Gwenllian

Edwina Hart

Vikki Howells

Jane Hutt

Julie James

Pauline Jarman

Delyth Jewell

Ann Jones

Elin Jones

Helen Mary Jones

Laura Anne Jones

Baroness Eluned Morgan

Julie Morgan

Lynne Neagle

Eluned Parrott

Rhianon Passmore

Baroness
Jenny Randerson

Jenny Rathbone

Janet Ryder

Antoinette Sandbach

Bethan Sayed

Karen Sinclair

Catherine Thomas

Gwenda Thomas

Joyce Watson

Kirsty Williams

Leanne Wood

ACKNOWLEDGEMENTS

A note on copyright

Image credits

The photographs of Hannah Blythyn, Michelle Brown, Eleanor Burnham, Jane Davidson, Jocelyn Davies, Sue Essex, Nerys Evans, Janice Gregory, Lesley Griffiths, Julie James, Ann Jones, Elin Jones, Laura Anne Jones, Lynne Neagle, Janet Ryder, Catherine Thomas, Gwenda Thomas and Joyce Watson are credited to and copyright of Comisiwn y Senedd/Senedd Commission. We are grateful to the staff of the Senedd Commission for providing these images.

The photographs of Jayne Bryant, Dawn Bowden, Angela Burns, Christine Chapman, Janet Davies, Suzy Davies, Tamsin Dunwoody, Delyth Evans, Lisa Francis, Veronica German, Siân Gwenllian, Edwina Hart, Vikki Howells, Jane Hutt, Pauline Jarman, Delyth Jewell, Helen Mary Jones, Julie Morgan, Eluned Morgan, Rhianon Passmore, Eluned Parrott, Jenny Randerson, Jenny Rathbone, Antoinette Sandbach, Bethan Sayed, Karen Sinclair, Kirsty Williams and Leanne Wood were taken during the project interviews and are copyright of Archif Menywod Cymru/Women's Archive Wales: credit Heledd Wyn Hardy and Catrin Edwards.

We have made every effort to ascertain the credit and copyright holder for the photograph of the 2003 Year of Parity Female Assembly Members, but without success. We have decided to include it here, nevertheless, due to its relevance to this volume and because it reflects such an important milestone in the history of the Assembly/Senedd and in the story of women in Welsh politics. If you have any information as to the photographer and/or copyright holder of this photograph, please contact Honno Press.

Translations

Of the interviews conducted during the project, ten of them were conducted through the medium of Welsh; namely Suzy Davies, Siân Gwenllian, Delyth Evans, Gwenda Thomas, Elin Jones, Nerys Evans, Delyth Jewell, Bethan Sayed, Eleanor Burnham and Eluned Morgan. All the extracts from these interviews, and the other thirty-six interviews conducted in English, which are included here have been translated accordingly and reproduced bilingually, in two volumes separately. Enormous thanks are due to Catrin Stevens for translating part of the English text to Welsh.

Sources

Oral interviews carried out with 48 AMs/MSs as part of the Women's Archive Wales project Setting the Record Straight, 2019-2021, 46 of which have been included here. Two have been omitted due to embargos placed on those particular interviews, namely Lorraine Barrett and Janet Finch-Saunders. Two interviews carried out with four members of the Youth Parliament have also been omitted.

As well as the above-mentioned images, we are very grateful to Senedd Cymru-Welsh Parliament for permission to reproduce from its website (https://senedd.wales/) the text used in the Appendices on Devolution in Wales, part of the Glossary of Political Terms, and some of the biographies; for the latter, thanks also go to Wikipedia.

John Osmond, Critical Mass: The Impact and Future of Female Representation in the National Assembly for Wales can be found at: https://www.iwa.wales/wp-content/media/2016/03/criticalmasseng.pdf

FOREWORD

In 2003, the Welsh National Assembly led the world. The legislature of Wales was the first in the world to achieve parity and an equal balance between the sexes as regards representation in its National democratic institution. That was an incredible feat, especially considering that only four female Members of Parliament had represented Wales in the United Kingdom Parliament between 1918 and 1997. The desire to mark this tremendous change, and give the contribution of women to our new democracy a lasting memorial, inspired the pioneering project that is reflected in this volume. In 2019, the National Assembly/Senedd was twenty years old – an important milestone in the history of the nation – and so it was deemed necessary to proceed with urgency to capture and preserve this history, while it was within living memory.

And so, the 'Setting the Record Straight / Gwir Gofnod o Gyfnod' project was launched by Archif Menywod Cymru / Women's Archive Wales to safeguard and preserve the papers and voices of women in Welsh politics. The main aim of the Archive is to raise awareness of the history of women in Wales and safeguard the sources of that history, because without sources we don't have a history. We facilitate the preserving of these sources by directing them to be deposited in county archives and in the National Library of Wales. This project met these aims perfectly. When the launch was held in the Assembly as part of the 2019 International Women's Day celebrations, through the sponsorship of the Deputy

Presiding Officer, Ann Jones, the main emphasis was on preserving the women's political papers and memorabilia. Research had shown that women were far more reluctant to appreciate their papers and safeguard them for the future than their male co-members. As a result, there was a scarcity of archives relating to female AMs/MSs in our local and national archives. It was realised that unless this situation was rectified, researchers and others who wished to study the political history of Wales during the formative years of the National Assembly/Senedd would get a distorted picture of the reality of the political situation.

But then the Archive was invited to meet members of the National Assembly Commission and we were urged to add the collecting of the oral histories of former and current AMs to the project, to ensure a fuller and more personal picture of the first years of devolution. This much more challenging and complex project was submitted to the National Lottery Heritage Fund, with a generous matching grant from the Welsh Government, in 2019. We were delighted when the proposal was accepted, and the work started in November 2019.

To run this ambitious venture, a team came together led by Dr Chris Chapman, former AM for Cwm Cynon and Chair of Women's Archive Wales, and comprising the Chief Executive of the Assembly, Manon Antoniazzi; the Llywydd and Deputy Presiding Officer: Elin Jones and Ann Jones; together with two officers, Enfys Roberts and Elin Roberts; Robert Phillips of the Welsh Political Archive in the National Library of Wales; Susan Edwards / Laura Cotton representing Glamorgan Archives; Dr Beth Thomas of the Oral History Society; and members of Woman's Archive Wales' committee: Mari James, Dr Dinah Evans, Gail Allen / Jane Davidson, treasurers; and Catrin Stevens – Project Coordinator. Officers were immediately appointed to put the project into action: Catrin Edwards in charge of filming oral histories; Heledd Wyn Hardy film-maker; and Kate Sullivan, Finance Officer, political papers and transcripts.

Despite all the dire difficulties of Covid 19, which halted the holding of face-to-face interviews and visiting archival offices, the work went ahead very successfully. As an Archive we owe these dedicated and inspired officers a huge debt. But Welsh history owes them an invaluable debt too. Catrin Edwards and Kate Sullivan, as you see, are responsible for this volume as well – another great favour. Thanks is due too to the small army of volunteers that transcribed the interviews to make them accessible to everyone.

So, what was achieved? Certainly, awareness was raised of the importance of safeguarding the political papers of women that record their experiences and their contributions to the Welsh Assembly/Senedd, and our local and national archives are richer as a result. As regards recording their voices, we succeeded in filming the histories of 48 of the 62 who had served during the first twenty years of devolution. Inevitably, we had to acknowledge that some had already died, others were too ill, and others were reluctant to contribute and share their experiences for various reasons. Yet, the response was truly positive, with many interviewees congratulating and thanking AMC/WAW for this initiative and greatly appreciating the opportunity to explore and describe their political experiences. We thank them for their support and for speaking so openly and interestingly about their lives and careers. This volume is a tribute to them.

This valuable book gives us only a glimpse of the incredible richness of the interviews, but the complete archive is now available for others to delve into in the Welsh National Screen and Sound Archive. The interviews were recorded on video – a medium that can enlighten us as well if not better sometimes than the spoken word. The topics discussed are wide-ranging and highly revealing: who were their political influences and how difficult was it to be selected to stand, in the face of the prejudices of the period; the challenges of the growth of social media; and did gender equality in the National Assembly/Senedd give rise to a different style of debate in the Chamber. One very significant theme was the campaigns led by the female AMs/MSs: free doctors' prescriptions in the Welsh NHS; the establishment of the Children's Commission; legislation in favour of water sprinklers in new homes; the campaign against physical violence and restraint; the Future Generations Act; the removal of sexist language in the legal and various documents of the Welsh Assembly/Senedd. They can be truly proud of this record.

It was a privilege to be involved in this innovative project. The 'Setting the Record Straight / Gwir Gofnod o Gyfnod' project has raised the profile of women in Welsh politics forever, through their political papers and their own unique words. Read, reflect and marvel at their dedication, their resilience and their vision.

CATRIN STEVENS
January 2023

Chapter One

BEGINNINGS AND FIRST IMPRESSIONS

The call for devolution in Wales had grown steadily in the 1980s and 1990s, and on 18 September, 1997, a referendum was held that showed a vote of 50.3 per cent in favour of a National Assembly for Wales. The following year, the Government of Wales Act provided the legal ground for such an Assembly, which would have the power to make secondary legislation in specific areas only, such as agriculture, education and housing.

The Assembly met for the first time on 12 May, 1999, and the building was officially opened by Queen Elizabeth II on 26 May. Of the 60 newly elected members of this First Assembly, 24 were women, an important shift in the history of a political arena in Wales which had been hitherto dominated by men.

In this first section of this book, we hear from some of the women who had the privilege and the responsibility to be the first female politicians to sit in the first ever Welsh Assembly, and in subsequent Assemblies, up to the celebration of its first twenty years in 2019.

PAULINE JARMAN

'My first impression was one of achievement for each of us, irrespective of political party. I felt we had a big responsibility as an organisation to really get some of the things that we so desperately needed delivered. And that was my impatience. It was so new; everything was so new. I had done a sort of apprenticeship in local government, so I was well used to some of the things that other colleagues weren't, like rules of debate, standing orders, points of order, all these things. I suppose those who were formerly MPs were also very familiar with it. So, it was an alien environment, but I'm a people watcher, and I'm inclined to take my time, get to know the territory, get to know the individuals, I don't form early judgements on anyone, I sit there and look and listen. We were all new to it and we could all have been lookers and listeners for a very long time. Was I in awe? I don't know if I was in awe, but I was certainly very proud to be sat there amongst the first 60 people to be given that very serious responsibility of looking after Wales and its affairs and delivering for its people in whatever small way I could. That was the pride that I felt.'

JANE DAVIDSON

'My first impression of the National Assembly was arriving in an underground car park in Crickhowell House, a building that had been built in the context of the Health Service that had been hastily adapted to become the new National Assembly for Wales. I remember arriving and being allocated to my car parking space and then getting out and a person was waiting for me by the door. And that person was Craig Stevenson, who went on to become my private secretary, both in my first role in the National Assembly as Deputy Presiding Officer and then as a Minister in the government. Craig was "buddied up" to me, as a member of the Civil Service, to help me as a new Assembly Member understand my way around the new institution. So, of course, I had to go and do all the things that new Assembly Members had to do. I had to be allocated a room. I had to be allocated a computer. I had to go and sign a declaration in terms of becoming an Assembly Member. I had to find out where the canteen was, where the toilets were – all the really important things in life! I remember Craig telling me on that first day how they had no idea what it was going to be like, in a sense, meeting real politicians, because they'd been through a series of exercises as members of the Civil Service about what it *might* be like but neither they, nor many of us, because many of us had never been politicians before, had any idea what it was going to be like walking through those doors.'

ELEANOR BURNHAM

'A huge honour and pleasure, but a shock and a fright, because I had been focussing on doing my best in Chester, being a JP, looking after the children, etc. First impressions – my sense of smell is quite acute, and the first thing was feeling rather sick because of the smell of Brain's [brewery] coming off the train. No-one wanted to help me, after all I'm an adult, but I didn't know anyone in the party, didn't know anyone in the group – they all came from Cardiff and the friendliest person was Mick Bates. So I didn't have any idea, and had to find that out in a hurry: how to do it, where to do it, and with whom to do it. I remember getting lost, going down in the lift, and not being able to come back up because everyone had gone home and I was on my own in the car park, and of course I didn't have a car because I'd travelled by train. The Chamber was small and every time a person coughed, everyone caught a cold!'

JENNY RANDERSON

'The serious point, the serious reason why I was pleased to do it, was it was so exciting. A new institution. We had to make up the rules. The people who became the first AMs, they had various backgrounds. There was Lord Dafydd Elis-Thomas, who of course had the Commons and the Lords in his background; there were several MPs; there were a lot of us who'd been councillors and knew how local councils worked; and there were people who'd never done it before. And we all came to it from a totally different perspective and formed what we saw as a new democracy. And I think some of our experiments worked, some were a failure. But the good thing was there was no-one standing there saying, "You can't do that because we always do so and so." There was none of the precedent. There was none of the rules set down by our forefathers. It was down to us. And we realised quite early on that we needed much more power.'

KIRSTY WILLIAMS

'I certainly had not anticipated how all-encompassing the job would be and how you would never be off duty. Even things that wouldn't be an issue for your average twenty-eight-year-old suddenly became an issue because you had this particular role. People used to make assumptions all the time about [me] not having enough experience, not being good enough, and I just felt that I had to work even harder to prove that somebody young – or younger, because twenty-eight isn't that young really – deserved to be there and could do that job. I can't even begin to imagine what it would have been like to go to Parliament in those circumstances. Although there were hugely experienced people in that Assembly in 1999, people who had long and very successful parliamentary careers in a Westminster context, people who'd had long and very successful careers in local government in Wales, because it was new in many ways it was almost like everybody was starting from scratch. I was hugely fortunate to go into that new institution where nobody could pull rank in that sense of having been there before. It was new for everybody. Nobody was quite sure how it would all work, nobody was quite sure what we should all do. There wasn't that weight of history in that sense upon us because, "Oh, that's how we've always done it." We were creating history as a group of people and you certainly felt that way, because the referendum margins had been so narrow. Certainly, I was acutely aware that we had to make it work, it had to be good, we had to prove to people that we had the right to be there, that the right decision had been made. It was terrifying, exciting, bewildering, overwhelming, just a huge sense of pride at simply getting there.'

DELYTH EVANS

'I think my strongest impression is that everything was new, an unusual, exciting new venture, and it was a brilliant experience to be part of that. But thinking of it now that people are used to the Assembly, it was something completely new in the governance of Wales, the governance of Britain. Not only a change for the people who were part of it, namely the members and the officers and the civil servants – of course that was very new for them – but it was also completely new for all the public bodies in Wales and the local authorities and anyone else who had to deal with the government. All these bodies had always been used to being led from London – the money, the budget, rules, everything coming from London – and suddenly, everything was happening in Wales. Therefore, it was the newness of everything, and the change that came in the wake of devolution was a huge thing for the whole of Wales and for public life to deal with. There was this feeling that people were learning on the job, learning as they went along, working out how to do things, how to behave, how to deal with problems. I was very aware of that process, people trying to work out how to make things work at all levels. On a personal level, politicians trying to learn the job, trying to work out how to contribute; at committee level, what their role was, the officers trying to adapt their way of working instead of looking to London for guidance, and trying to take that guidance from Cardiff; local authorities trying to work out how they fitted in, [what] their relationships were with the different bodies they worked with. It was a huge change – a revolution in a way. So, when trying to remember what people's objectives were in that first period, I think the most important thing was just trying to establish it and lay down roots and make the Assembly acceptable and credible to people in Wales.'

LYNNE NEAGLE

'And then I suppose I felt a bit daunted. I'd pushed myself to do it and then you suddenly think, "Oh, gosh, I've got to do this job now." I'd never really done anything like this. So, I remember feeling very scared afterwards and suddenly thinking, "Oh my goodness, you've got to have to stand up now and make speeches, you're going to have to do all these things that you've never done before." I was lucky in a way, though, because my husband was also elected as the AM for Merthyr Tydfil and Rhymney and I did have that inbuilt support there from the start really, that lots of young women in my position wouldn't have had. It was very friendly, it was exciting, everybody was very pleased because there were so many women in the Labour Group, so it felt like a new start in that sense. And it was just a lot to take in really. I just remember concentrating really hard, trying to remember where I needed to be, to not allow myself to become too overawed by it really. I was the youngest member of the Labour Group then and it was lucky I had the support of my husband, because I think I would have felt much more overwhelmed if there hadn't been two of us – because it was new for him as well – trying to navigate all the new systems.'

ANN JONES

'It doesn't seem almost 22 years ago. I remember travelling down with Karen Sinclair, whom I knew from being a county councillor. I remember going in on the first morning, which was the Tuesday morning, and we walked in, and I said to Karen, "This is it! We're going to change the world!" And the next two days, I did nothing but move from room to room, getting lost around the building, and just talking to loads of lobbyists and organisations and people who wanted to tell us why we should support their particular manifestos. I remember saying to Karen, "Well we haven't set the world alight, have we?" And she went, "No, I don't think so!" But I think it was the aspiration that we were here. We were the new kids on the block, and we were going to do all of this. Actually, it didn't really work like that. You were allocated your office, and finding the post room, and getting the post. And I remember a couple of weeks later – Alison Halford had been elected the member for Delyn – and we were sitting having a cup of tea in the canteen. And I said to Karen, "Oh, have you had this?" And Alison said, "What are you two finding to work on? I haven't had any post." So, Karen took her, metaphorically by the hand, to the post room, and Alison's pigeonhole was overflowing. She thought the post would be brought to her, because she was Assistant Chief Constable when she left the police, and you opened the Chief Officer's mail and you sorted it out, so she was working on that assumption. So, it was just things like that. But everybody was new, with the exception of Rhodri Morgan, who'd come from being an MP, Alun Michael, Ieuan Wyn [Jones], Dafydd Wigley, Dafydd Elis-Thomas, Ron Davies. The rest of us, it was a new experience.'

JANE HUTT

'As far as the Assembly was concerned, we just knew that we were the new ones and that we were actually going to make it work. It was our responsibility. It wasn't an impression *of* the Assembly, *we were* the Assembly, it wasn't about buildings. And it was also very quick. Within days, I was appointed Health and Social Services Minister, so we barely had time to be given a room. I had been an elected representative, as a councillor before, so it wasn't new to me being an elected representative, and I'd been involved in the 'Yes for Wales' Campaign. Lots of colleagues came in, people, friends I knew came into the Assembly with me. But we realised we had a huge task ahead of us.'

CHRISTINE CHAPMAN

'There was a sense of new beginnings, a new culture. Looking back now, I really underestimated what the job would entail. Not so much the job but the profile. I really underestimated the publicity and profile we had around it. The first week it felt like the world's press were there. The *Daily Mirror* did a feature and they picked on me for some reason, took a picture of me in my office, and they wanted to know about the first few days of an AM. The first day I turned up in an empty office, nothing on my desk, no staff, and you think, "Gosh, I've got to employ staff, I've got to get a constituency office," so there were all these practical things to do. But once those things were in place, things started to work out. You'd wake up in the morning and the first thing you'd think about was, you're there, you're an Assembly Member. And I remember driving to work and I'd constantly have Radio Wales on, you could never switch off, you wanted to know what was going on. I felt, for quite a few years actually, that you could just not switch off; it's very difficult to switch off anyway when you're a politician. But it was really exciting as well, setting up, being on a committee, being lobbied by so many people. I think in the early days you almost say yes to everything, and I learnt over the course of the next few years that you've got to be much more discerning about what you do.'

JAYNE BRYANT

Jayne had worked there thirteen years previously, as staff to Rosemary Butler, before becoming an AM herself in 2016:

'Strangely, I had the office that Rosemary had, so it was quite funny being sat in the same room! Things had changed and got better. The whole process, when you go and take your oath, was a wonderful process. I actually changed my oath to include "for the people of Newport West", which I'm not sure people realise you could do, but that was something I felt very strongly about. A feeling that things had really changed, that it had grown, I suppose. It does feel like there's another mountain to climb because you don't want to let people down, going into it. I knew the building and my way around it, and I still knew some of the people who worked there. But it's just a different role. I went into it with my eyes open, as somebody who'd worked there previously, somebody who'd worked for an MP who was very active and busy, but the workload is significantly more than I thought it would be. Obviously, I knew it's not a 9–5 role but just the amount of committee work – and at the start I was actually on three committees – and I went in thinking I'd read around the subjects every time and then quickly realised that, to get through the papers, was a tough enough job. So, a lot of work but I really enjoy it.'

LISA FRANCIS

'I thought it was very well organised. I was amazed by the amount of help I was offered. Members' research facilities – it was amazing to have that resource available. Our Presiding Officer, Dafydd

Elis-Thomas, and Deputy, John Marek were very experienced people who were very keen to put the welfare of their people first. Dafydd particularly was something of a beacon in that he firmly believed that all members should be treated equally, regional and constituency. He absolutely believed that to his core, whereas a lot of the Labour Members didn't really like the fact that the Conservatives at the time had done really well on the regional list, it had given them a platform they hadn't had before. I think there was quite a lot of resentment about that. But I was impressed by the whole organisation, maybe that was because it was new, I don't know. I was slightly overwhelmed. I couldn't quite believe how different my life had become in the space of a few months. And there were times when I fully expected somebody to tap me on the shoulder and say, "It's all been a terrible mistake, you really shouldn't be here!" That was because I'd got in on a wing and prayer and that kind of stays with you.'

KAREN SINCLAIR

'As well as excitement, there was a lot of trepidation. All of the women, certainly in our Labour group, did meet together and support one another, particularly Rosemary Butler who sort of saw herself as our mum, I think, which we actually did need at the time because it was just such a huge upheaval. You won the election on the Thursday and by the Tuesday – well, by the Monday because of travelling – you were off to Cardiff. There was no time to actually make big plans about how you were going to do it. And I well remember Ann Jones and I, we were in a hotel, neither of us were familiar with Cardiff, we'd driven down, and we hadn't got a clue where we were going to stay, so we stopped at a hotel just off the M4 quite late at night. And Alun Michael rang and had a chat and he actually said, "Where are you, Karen?" And I said "I've got no idea! I'm in a hotel somewhere off the M4." That was so funny at the time, but looking back, it's even more hilarious really. Going in and all introducing ourselves to one another, it was quite amazing and a huge privilege. People don't tend to think about that, but I do think it is a privilege. But I did take a decision very early on that I wanted to do my speeches from a seated position and that's because I always thought standing was almost an aggressive act in Parliament where there used to be the opposition over here and the Government over there and they'd stand up and have a bit of a bash about. And I thought that was sad really, it was more political theatre rather than actually getting things done and I've never been into political theatre in the chamber. People did get a little bit cross about it [her speaking sitting down]. Dafydd El [Lord Elis-Thomas] didn't worry at all but other people were a bit shocked by it. But I still did it and the more people mentioned it, the more I did it because I felt it actually made a statement that we could do things without standing up and being adversarial with one another.'

* * *

Chapter Two

POLITICAL INFLUENCES AND ROLE MODELS

The female Assembly Members who were elected to the First Assembly in 1999, and in subsequent years, came from varying backgrounds. Some had been councillors, some had worked for politicians, some had been involved in pressure groups and various political or quasi-political campaigns, including the 'Yes for Wales' drive for a national assembly. Some had had no political background at all to speak of, and many said they'd never thought of becoming, or ever expected to become, a politician. Most of those interviewed spoke of role models and mentors, political and otherwise, that shaped their beliefs and thinking, helped them along various career paths, and often inspired, and even dictated, their decision to stand for election, as detailed in the following section.

HANNAH BLYTHYN

'I think like many of my generation I was probably politicised by what happened in the major industries of the area. My granddad was at Shotton Steelworks and was made redundant and it's him I vaguely remember talking to me about politics and trade unions and things like that. I never thought I would be a politician because I didn't think it was something for somebody like me. Generally, politicians didn't look like me, nor anybody I knew. What I realised when I was younger, certain things I did *were* political but not what you'd see in a party-political sense. At my second junior school, we staged a sit-in because girls weren't allowed to wear trousers, then. It was never resolved in my time but now when I go back and visit, they can actually wear trousers. I just remember complaining about things once and my mum saying to me, "Well, Hannah, you can either do something about it, you can moan it's not fair or you can actually get up and do something about it." So, I was influenced by family but outside of the family, I couldn't pin any one role model, but I guess anybody who was prepared to stick their head up above the parapet, [who] perhaps wouldn't be the obvious contender to be a politician, perhaps a little bit further afield. If you look at things in the States, things like Harvey Milk and the Stonewall Riots, and things like that. I guess people who have gone through the Labour Movement at a UK level, so maybe people like Barbara Castle, people that you perhaps see as the underdog who have really challenged those injustices, and may not have overcome them overnight, but over time have created some change.'

JANICE GREGORY

'In terms of role models, in the constituency in Ogmore, there was a wonderful, wonderful woman who would have loved to have participated in this project. Her name was Muriel Williams.

She was the daughter of a miner, the wife of a miner, lived in a small mining village called Nant-y-moel, and she was an absolute force to be reckoned with. She became a councillor when it wasn't fashionable for women to be councillors, and she was fantastic, she was fearless, she knew her stuff, she knew her politics, she knew her roots, and she always treated everyone the same. The stories of her in what was then Ogmore Borough Council and her put-downs of opposition, especially Tory opposition councillors, is legend. She was wonderful and she was a role model without realising she was a role model.'

SUE ESSEX

'[Mine] wasn't a political family in that sense. There was that wider politics that, say, my parents would have been horrified at voting to come out of Europe, there was that wider politics that the war gave them. My grandparents growing up in the Depression, my mother being a child of the Depression, seeing her small siblings die of children's diseases. So, there was the politics of that. There certainly wasn't "party politics" in the way that we would know it now, but it was that politics of the goodness in ordinary people if they are only given a chance. I don't think I had role models as such. I used to read a lot, I used to keep an eye on all the things that were going on. I used to talk to anyone who, like me, was a bit interested. It really was when I went to Leicester University. Dipak Nandy was there and so we started to have the first anti-apartheid demonstrations. I think we had the first one there at Leicester, or certainly the first one that Dipak organised, the first of those. And that I think was a very important movement for young people my age, of understanding that things had got better for us in the UK, because they had. It was early '60s, all the opportunities, that was an amazing change from the '50s to the early '60s. You know, there was music, there were clothes, a bit more money around, but also the scourge of apartheid suddenly came and smacked us in the face, in a way that we didn't know. So that was quite influential but still I suppose ... my roots ... I suppose were always in my working-class community.'

LEANNE WOOD

'My grandmother was a great role model for me. She was born in 1920, so her growing up memories were in the 1930s, and that in terms of my politics – I look back now, I didn't see it at the time – but the stories that she told about growing up in the Rhondda, being sent to London to work in service for wealthy families, being in London when the Blitz happened. There was one very poignant story that she told me where most of her money had to be sent back home, to look after her siblings, she was one of nine, and she was one of the oldest, and she was desperate for a winter coat. So, she'd found a coat that she wanted in a window, went into the shop, put money down on it, to buy it – over a period of time, you'd pay the money off and then you'd get the coat. And by the time she'd paid the money off, the coat was too small. She used to cry every time she told me that story, [of her] at the age of fourteen, fifteen and she still felt the pain 50 or 60 years later. For me that kind of sums up the poverty, the desperation, the difficult time, people like her and her generation lived through, and it puts into perspective some of the problems faced today. Also, I had a fantastic teacher, my history teacher in school, Mr Richard Gamman. He was somebody who just made us think things in a different way. He would always get us to challenge convention. If there was something in a book that was stated as fact, he would get us to question the sources of that information, whether it was factual or not. And having a teacher who just made you question convention and received wisdom, for me was an absolute liberation. We don't have a great wealth of women politicians from the Valleys to draw upon. One of the reasons I was drawn into politics, actually, was because, growing up, up there were very few people I felt representing me, and whether that was in literature or on the television, in the news or in politics, there were just so very few. So, part of the motivation for getting involved in politics was an absence of those role models. So, I had to look elsewhere. I looked a lot to America, actually, for role models, and found a lot of them in writers from the South, black women from the South, people like Alice Walker, Toni Morrison, Marge Piercy – not a black writer, but a Jewish socialist from America. These were the places where I found I drew my political inspiration, from the pages of literature in a different country.'

ANTOINETTE SANDBACH

'We weren't a political family. I had a great uncle, whom I never knew, who was elected as an MP, on my grandfather's side, his brother, but he died long before I was born. Other than that, I wasn't aware of anyone in the family being in politics, and I think I'm the first woman elected in the family. I was growing up when Margaret Thatcher was Prime Minister and therefore it seemed very usual that a woman *could* be Prime Minister. But, having been in Downing Street and having walked up that yellow staircase, which has endless portraits of men, you realise how unusual her achievement was, and really how extraordinary it was. But I suppose, because of when I was born, I was a teenager when she was Prime Minister, so she definitely gave the impression that women could get involved in that arena. But that was perhaps subconscious, because I went to work as a legal aid lawyer, I always thought I would carry on working as a legal aid lawyer. I only started getting more political when I became a single mum.'

EDWINA HART

'I think it's very difficult to talk about political role models because my heart was always, and will always be actually, within the trade union movement rather than in politics. When I finished school, I went, briefly, to university but wasn't very happy. I liked the world of work. I liked having money in my pocket. I took a job, which I should really never have taken, and of course, joined the trade union from that. So, it was the trade union movement, I think, that had the greatest influence on me. I always remember when I went to my first national TUC conference. There were not that many women there, and you looked at the platform and you recognised Marie Patterson from the Transport and General Workers Union, Pat Turner from the GMB, and there were so few of them. But the women that you met through the trade union movement were exceptionally supportive of you in what you wanted to do. They always remembered you, you always talked to them, you had a relationship with them, and those were probably my role models, the women that really fought to get equal pay, wanted to do things, and wanted to change the world from the perspective of women.'

GWENDA THOMAS

'Well, I think Mam and Dad, to tell the truth. I was born into the Labour Party. It wasn't something you thought about, it was natural. They were always going to meet up with others who were quite active politically. Looking back, there were a number of people. Harold Wilson, I used to listen to him a great deal, and how he fought two general elections, he influenced me greatly. And of course, I was always hearing about Keir Hardie, all these as I was growing up. Barbara Castle, I thought a lot about her because she strove to get women's toilets in the Houses of Commons, because there was nothing for women before this, nowhere for women to do what they wanted to do, see to their personal needs. Then to see the place had been called "Barbara's Castle"! I thought that was great – those sorts of women. I don't think women always support other women, but I have to say that I had strong support from men, especially when I became a member of West Glamorgan County Council. There were two leaders – Tom Jones and Fred Kingdom, at the time – who showed faith in me, who hadn't been elected more than three years, and then became the Chair of the Social Services Committee. No woman had ever chaired such a committee before this. I have to admit to the support I received from men too.'

JAYNE BRYANT

'When I was about nine, I was at St Julian's Primary School, and Paul Flynn had just got elected to Newport West. I lived in Newport East, but Paul was able to come to my school, as some of his constituents went there. I remember my parents telling me this was such a big thing – "Paul Flynn, new MP, is going to come to your school," – and I can still remember where I was sat. Meeting a politician for the first time was pretty special, and something that I feel is really important is that politicians get out and speak and are seen and heard in their communities, so that people think that it is achievable. Paul was one of the big influences even from a young age. And I was very much interested in the environment, so from about eleven/twelve, I started getting interested in the ozone layer and recycling, and that really sort of took me down one path. So, I felt quite politicised from a young age, even though I obviously wasn't involved at that age in a party-political guise.'

BETHAN SAYED

'When I was growing up – my mother came from Northern Ireland originally – so I found it interesting discussing that and visiting Belfast to see what was happening there. In the 1980s, it was still difficult politically there, there was a lot of violence, but she inspired me, since she'd come from such a difficult place to grow up and had come to Wales to escape this. People speak of Palestine and Lebanon, etc, but bombs went off every day on the streets of Belfast, and I read a great deal about this and looked up to people like Bobby Sands, who had done a lot for the cause from the standpoint of the Republic, and people like De Valera in the Republic, who had fought for a united Ireland. So, when I was young, I looked to Ireland, and also to someone like Nelson Mandela, because I did a lot with anti-apartheid campaigns, and I was inspired by this too. But there weren't many great political figures when I was growing up. In my teens I wasn't involved in politics. I was more into music and orchestras. When I went to college, I took part in more of these campaigns and found people in the SNP, like Nicola Sturgeon, someone I looked up to, and Leanne Wood, who came to Aberystwyth when I was in college, with Dafydd Iwan. And I saw a politician who looked like me, who sounded like me, and someone who appealed to me when I hadn't really looked at party politics before this.'

MICHELLE BROWN

'In terms of activism the family wasn't active politically. None of my family have ever stood for election, as far as I know. But there was always an interest in politics and current affairs. When I was a child, the news was on almost constantly in the background. My grandparents were well educated, and they would argue with the politicians, a lot of talking back to the TV in my family when I was a child, and I still do it. There was one recently that has been put up as being a role model for modern girls although it has caused quite a stir, but a major heroine of mine as a child of seven or eight was Wonder Woman. I came from a Conservative family so when Margaret Thatcher became Prime Minister, it was influential on me as a girl in a Conservative family. She had become Prime Minister and she was making the big decisions. Whatever you think of her politics, she achieved something that feminism was trying to achieve, equality in politics. Here was a woman who was a real strong woman, strong enough to fight her way through a very patriarchal political system and become Prime Minister. I was nine when Margaret Thatcher went into Number 10 and I was twenty when she left, so my entire teenage years were under a female Prime Minister who very much bucked the trend for women, particularly at the time. Shirley Williams as well. I don't agree with her politics, but I greatly admired Shirley Williams for much the same reasons.'

LAURA ANNE JONES

'When I eventually joined the Conservative Party, I went along to my first meeting in Usk, at the Conservative Club, where the average age was probably about eighty, and I said, "What I am doing here?" I was fifteen years of age at that point. But two people there became very big influences in my political life. One was Peter Davies, who was the biggest, my mentor. He was an amazing man. He was very forthright, very welcoming to me, and took me under his wing, and immediately took me up to the Gurnos Estate in Merthyr canvassing. I think he was testing me to see how I'd fare, really. I had dogs set on me, doors slammed in my face as a Tory, but I loved it. All those people that I'd just made *think* about the fact that they had a choice in politics, they didn't have to vote Labour because their grandparents did, they could think about their children's futures, and they could help shape it by voting a different way. So, he really developed me in the importance of talking to people. I saw him on the doorstep adapting how he approached people of all ages, all backgrounds. I really learned a lot from him about how to communicate with people. There was someone else there that night called Audrey Hull and she was the woman in the party. She was extremely strong, Margaret Thatcher-esque in her presence, and everything else, in the way she dressed and the way she conducted herself and the way she was respected by men and women alike. I thought, "Wow, this woman's a power-house and one day I'd like to be like that, she's really done it." So, those two people, and, of course, Margaret Thatcher, another powerful woman, and it just proved to me that it was possible.'

SUZY DAVIES

'From a political viewpoint, the first woman I remember is Barbara Castle, of course. From an influential viewpoint – I know you're all thinking I'm going to name Margaret Thatcher. In a way, she was emblematic, she was the first [female] Prime Minister, of course – but the one who made me think of politics perhaps was Mo Mowlam. Of course, she comes from a different party, but what struck me was the way she was willing to speak to everyone. Not quite informally but not quite in the old-fashioned way we used to see before that. It's disappointing that she didn't quite get the credit for what happened in Northern Ireland, well, the whole of Ireland. Perhaps Tony Blair felt a little jealous of how she'd been so successful in doing what she did and took more of the credit than perhaps was fair. Of course, she wasn't the first one to do work in Ireland. I have to say that John Major made some sort of influence there. But not quite "under the radar", and that, of course, is how politics can work in the best way.'

VIKKI HOWELLS

'I think a lot of it arose from my love of local history, and particularly growing up in the South Wales Valleys, when you're interested in your history, you can't help but to be imbued with politics as you look into that and the struggle of the working classes, particularly in the coal mining areas, against the coal owners. I think that's what really got me thinking and shaped my thinking. And I also remember very clearly, when I was seven, it was the Miner's Strike in 1984, and a lot of the children in my class, their parents, their fathers were miners, their mothers were helping out with all of that. I certainly remember my mother answering the door to other women that we knew in the village who were asking if there was any food that we could donate. And I remember there were certain of my friends' mothers were very active in that. Even at that young age, I had this impression that women were at the forefront of something that was very important. I remember seeing on the news about children who wouldn't be having Christmas presents because of the Miner's Strike. That was the moment I realised there was no Father Christmas and it made me really cross because it was the politics that had really destroyed that myth for me. And I took that quite seriously in my own little head, aged seven, and started to really listen to the news a lot more and that developed into just enjoying discussing politics with anybody I could find who was interested. And when I was seventeen, my mother said to me, "What would you like for Christmas, Victoria?" and I said, "I'd like membership of the Labour Party, please." And my parents thought I had totally lost the plot! They thought that was the strangest gift their seventeen-year-old daughter could ask for. There was an incident that triggered me, thinking, "Right, I really want to join the Labour Party," and that was the buyout of Tower Colliery by the miners, and the involvement of Ann Clwyd. And I remember watching that unfold on a daily basis and being very impressed that there was such passion in the local community, and that people here were doing something that hadn't been done anywhere else in the world before, to buy their own mine and to run it. So that was a big influence on me, and Ann was a big influence in regard to that as well.'

JOCELYN DAVIES

'My mother's first cousin is Llew Smith, the Labour MEP and MP, who was also from Newbridge, so politics had been in my mother's side of the family and also on my father's side of the family, but of course that was Labour. But in the 1960s, my mother and father both joined Plaid Cymru. I was still in primary school, and, in that part of Wales, that was not the most popular choice. But they were disillusioned with local politics, both nationalists in believing that Wales should have its own parliament, and they greatly admired the local Plaid Cymru politicians. Aneurin Richards was our local councillor, and he was seen as a man with extreme integrity. He was a "good guy". They liked him, they liked his message and so they joined the party. I was about nine. Aneurin regularly turned up at the house with leaflets that I have to tell you *they* didn't deliver – me and my brother were usually dispatched to deliver these leaflets around the doors. And at that time Plaid Cymru had a "family membership", so for a certain fee you all signed up. So, we had family membership and considered ourselves, even from quite young children really, as part of a Plaid Cymru family. Aneurin was the main focus. Aneurin was the same age as my father. Even just before his death, which was just a couple of years ago, people in Newbridge were still talking about him. You don't meet many people like Aneurin Richards in your life. He was just one of those people that always wanted to do the right thing, he was absolutely committed to this cause, and he was so supportive of me. And sometimes women need a man to tell them that they can do it, that has been the theme actually throughout my life. Ironically, the encouragement of a man that you admire can give you the confidence to do something that your friends have been telling you that you can do. And Aneurin was certainly one of my influences. When I stood in the by-election, a lot of Plaid Cymru Members came to Islwyn to help. I started going to National Council, so I then met other women who were in Plaid Cymru – Helen Mary Jones, Laura McAllister, Siân Edwards – people who, I suppose, I learnt so much from. They just seemed to me to be good people with integrity, and that's the thing that I admired a lot. Unfortunately, I didn't have any Welsh, so that was one aspect of it that I couldn't join in, but there was a kind of family feeling about it, and inside of that there was a little sisterhood that was also very attractive, and I felt very welcome there. They understood me.'

JULIE JAMES

'There are two teachers that particularly stick out to me. One was a teacher in a Northern Ontario school, and she took me under her wing a bit, because that was the twelfth or fourteenth school I'd been to. And in that school in Northern Ontario, we lived in a tiny place called Manitoba, a long way out in the Canadian Bush, in a small mining town. And there was what would now be called a First Nation's tribe living there, but at that time was called an American Indian tribe. And the children of that tribe were in the school with us, but they were completely segregated, like apartheid, in a completely different set of classes and so on. And I had asked this teacher about it, and she told me all about it and how outraged she was by the fact that they were being treated like that. I would have been about ten or eleven and it really changed the way I felt about school and all of that. And my love of history and the way you regard British colonialism was

24

completely changed just by this particular teacher's very liberal take on it, in the '60s, when it just wasn't on the radar for most white people that that was any kind of issue. When I came back to Britain and went to school in Penzance, when I was fourteen, I came across a history teacher, who was about the worst history teacher I've ever encountered in my life, who knew nothing about history and was teaching British colonial history as if the Empire was a magnificent thing. And she did me a huge favour because she taught me to argue. Because I hated what she was saying, and of course I started to argue with her in the class. So, she made me kind of argumentative and determined to stick to my guns.'

* * *

Chapter Three

STANDING FOR ELECTION

The women interviewed during our project followed various paths to the National Assembly-Senedd, both to the First Assembly in 1999, and in subsequent elections, and also to council seats before becoming an AM/MS. Some had been active in their local parties, some had been staff in previous Assemblies, or had worked in quasi-political organisations or pressure groups. One or two had already been serving in Parliament, while others had come via the trade union movement and local councils, and some had held down other jobs, as well, or ran their own businesses. Some of the women entered politics at a young age, fresh from university, or soon after, while others entered later in life, either having had little or no active interest in politics beforehand, or not being party-politically focused at all. Without exception, all the women interviewed expressed concern over the burning issues of the time and the need to address them, and all had a passion to change things in their local communities, their constituencies and in Wales. Here is a selection of some of the interesting, and often unusual routes that saw them enter political life.

JANE DAVIDSON

'I'd spent the whole of my time working both in the Welsh Local Government Association and for the National Local Government Forum against poverty, meeting people from all over the UK and putting a hand up and going, "actually it's not like that in Wales," and people would just say, "Oh, Wales doesn't matter because it's only five per cent of the population." But Wales *does* matter. As somebody living in Wales and knowing that Wales was the poorest part of the UK, and that government policies were not giving Wales what it needed, I just felt Wales mattered more than ever. And therefore, when the National Assembly came along, I was really disappointed that I couldn't stand. But, of course in Labour, what happened because of politics that I think were mostly behind the scenes but very much then became front and central – of enabling Alan Michael to come in as a candidate for Mid and West Wales, because he was looking to move from being a Member of Parliament to an Assembly Member – the list was opened. And so, literally, I saw on the news that the list was opened – I think it only stayed open for a couple of weeks – but I applied to that new list, and I became a *bona fide* Assembly candidate. This was only about three of four weeks before the list for Pontypridd opened, and that was the constituency I lived in and therefore I put my name forward for the Pontypridd Constituency. But when I entered the selection process in Pontypridd, I found I entered a selection process where the constituency Labour Party, the active members of the constituency Labour Party, the executive, had already decided on who their candidates for this were going to be. In their view, they were just going to have a selection, in partnership with Merthyr – that was the twinned constituency – which enabled the preferred candidates to come forward from Pontypridd and Merthyr. My entering the selection was a huge challenge to the mechanism that the executive had decided they wanted to follow. And it soon became clear that my entering the selection was viewed by a lot of people in the constituency Labour Party as a real breath of fresh air.'

TAMSIN DUNWOODY

'I'd actually gone to selections before that [in 2003], for the Westminster seats here in Wales, and they were quite controversial, because it was predominantly male candidates who were successful and particularly in the safe seats; women were only being successful in the marginal or swing seats. There were a number of issues where we were supposed to speak in a working men's club where women were banned. It was a very good learning experience, a good learning curve, and it taught you the process, literally – the creation of leaflets, delivering, talking to members, putting across your case, why you rather than the other six or seven people, and it's a very set procedure that you go through. Then the seat came up here for the Senedd [sic]. Because I was an active party member locally, I then put myself forward. [On election night] I had spent my entire childhood watching votes mounting up, so I was watching the votes mounting up and thinking, "I'm actually going to win this!" And, even though I saw it happening, it was still a shock. And I can remember for weeks afterwards driving across the Preseli Mountains and thinking to myself, "Oh my God, I'm the Assembly Member here!" It was very overwhelming.'

JULIE MORGAN

Julie was one of the women to have been a Welsh MP before the First Assembly elections in 1999:
'I'd fought Cardiff North in '92, and that was an open selection, and I won it. And then we made big progress in the votes but obviously didn't win. And then in '97, when it came up again, I thought I'd have another go there. I did have the opportunity to go other

places, though I don't know whether I'd have got them or not, but I thought it better to stick with the constituency. I'd got very fond of Cardiff North and the people there, so I decided I would have another go. In the first round, during the selection process, it was quite biased against women, for example, I was asked, "Who's going to look after your children if you go to Westminster?" and people were sometimes a bit sexist. Rhodri was an MP already and they would say to me, "Oh, I don't like Rhodri, so we don't want you," that sort of thing. But, nevertheless, I got that nomination, and we had a good campaign. But then when the next time came round, Cardiff North offered to be an all-women shortlist because it meant you could be selected much earlier. Because if you agreed in the Labour Party to have an all-women shortlist, they were so keen to get women that they were doing those first.'

JANET RYDER

'I remember being in a National Executive meeting and we were reviewing what was happening and we were looking at the names that were available. And all of a sudden, in the middle of this meeting, Wigley – as only Wigley can do it – banged his fists on the desk [and said], "We're stopping this process now!" And he points at me and says, "And you're putting your name forward." So, I wasn't really given much choice in it. I had to go through the whole process, because what had happened when we came to elect the list in North Wales, all these really good women had backed out, because they thought, "Well, there's no point." But once my name went in, thankfully, all these other women came in as well. So, there was a lot of good names, women, that competed for that North Wales list the first time round in '99. It was no given thing that I would be elected. I did happen to top the list, and I quite convincingly topped it as well, but I never set out to go into the Assembly. I remember polling day being a very long day, and halfway through, it really didn't look like I was going to be elected, because we'd got Gareth [Jones] elected in Conwy, and we thought, well, that's it really, three seats in North Wales shared into the vote probably meant I wouldn't get elected. But I did and I remember we'd arranged a bus that night that picked up along various places and we ended up in the Celtic Manor [sic] in Caernarfon, and that was quite a party that night, I don't remember coming home very much.'

ELUNED PARROTT

'The 2010 General Election came around. The selection process in my party is there'll be an advert that goes out, and I filled in an application form, applied, like you would for a job. Before that, before you can stand, there is a training and selection process so you can be an approved candidate. I hadn't yet gone through that at that point, so I was only able to be a candidate because I was approved on licence. So, I had an interview to talk about my Liberalism and to check that I was an okay person, and that I would not be a liability. And that was my first experience of an election campaign. Very much testing the water. I didn't expect to win. The Vale of Glamorgan is a marginal seat between Labour and the Conservatives. At that time, the previous Labour MP was stepping down and a new candidate had come forward, Alun Cairns – his election for the first time for this seat. What was really enjoyable about that process actually is there was no pressure at all. There were no expectations. I could just enjoy getting out and campaigning, talking about the things I cared about, going out and meeting people, knocking on doors, and going to a lot of hustings, there were a lot of hustings for that election, I think about eight. Some election campaigns there haven't been any, so being a contest seat, there were quite a lot. So, yes, that was an interesting experience.'

SUE ESSEX

'I was persuaded to stand for a councillor and stood for Riverside. Jane Hutt was there, Mark Drakeford came later, Rhodri Morgan became the MP, Jane Davidson became the AM – so wonderful experiences as councillor in Riverside and Pontcanna, second to nothing actually in terms of what we were doing and working together. Then, as a councillor, first I was Deputy Leader and then I had the chance to become the first woman leader of Cardiff Council, which was marvellous. And that again was a game changer really, in terms of making that point, but hopefully doing things that were good for women, and good for everyone. It was lovely, actually. I loved my time as a councillor. People were so supportive. The day after I got elected, I remember coming into that grand City Hall, in the marble hall there, and these wonderful women were always polishing the brass. One of them just stopped me and she said, "Sue, all the girls have asked me to say how proud they are of you." Well, it was the proverbial lump in the throat moment. "How proud we are of you. You are the first woman leader ever." And I said, "Does that matter to you?" – honestly these women were working their socks off. "Oh yes," she said. "Oh yes, it really matters to us. We are all so proud." And if I did it for nothing else, that was the moment that you think, actually, breaking through these glass ceilings, it's not really you, it's what you do and what message that sends out that's so critical.'

JENNY RATHBONE

'Members of the [Labour] Party asked me if I would be prepared to stand for the election in 2011, so it was just around the corner. I guess they had put off selecting a candidate because of the General Election. I thought that this was a really interesting idea. I hadn't really considered it up until then because I was focused on going into Parliament, but clearly devolution enabled Wales to make its own decisions about education, health, and public transport, and a lot of other things besides. But education and health were issues that I really cared passionately about and so I could see a lot of attraction in doing this. I really got into it. I did manage in that twelve-month period to turn it round and win the seat, partly because the indomitable Jenny Randerson, who had held the seat since 1999, was retiring. So, there was a new candidate who didn't have her track record. I think if it had been Jenny Randerson, I probably wouldn't have made it, just because she had incumbency. But she was moving off to the House of Lords, so I seized the opportunity and won on behalf of the Labour Party."

ANTOINETTE SANDBACH

'The Conservative Party at that time was very much changing. It was casting off its "bad image", its "nasty party image", and having thought that I would not be the kind of person that the Conservatives would like – I was a member of Amnesty International and Friends of the Earth, and I was at [the] time a single parent – I thought that I would not be an attractive candidate for the Conservative Party. But I was told that I was exactly what they were looking for. So I went back to Wales, because I was living in Wales at that time with my daughter, and I contacted the Clwyd West agent – Vince Morris, at that time – and he told me to fill in a form. So, I filled in the form and then he asked me lots of questions like, "How many doors have you knocked on?" and the answer was "None!" And I thought, well, I probably haven't got the experience, so I said, "Actually, I've probably made a mistake." But he said, "No, come in and see me." I went in my muddy jeans and my farm jacket, and he was very encouraging. So, I joined the Conservative Party on 28th March. I did my selection board on 6th April, and by the 7th of June that year [2006] I was the selected candidate in Delyn.'

ANGELA BURNS

'I think I was asked to stand for the Assembly because, in 2006, when my girls were teeny tiny, I went along to a couple of public meetings, because there was this "Designed to Deliver Programme", about changing Withybush Hospital, about closing the hospital, moving all the hospital things around. I read the document and was deeply, hugely unimpressed with it. And at one particular meeting in Pembroke, in the town hall, I really challenged the Health Board at the time and, basically, because of all the things I was saying, I got approached by various people saying would I consider helping the local group fight against the move. I think, having had a couple of kids, and Stuart and I had been a bit "gipsy" in our lives, and we kind of nested in Pembrokeshire, it became very much our home. We'd returned to roots we didn't know we had, and we put down roots we didn't know we were able to put down. We bedded into that community very strongly, we made a lot of friends. I'd been helping my neighbour, who needed to have dialysis and had to travel to Swansea for dialysis, and getting in the local school, and suddenly you stop looking at the really huge picture and you look at the much smaller picture, which is your community and the people that surround you. And I thought, hang on a minute! Our school is falling down. If you close this hospital, where's everyone going to go? Our roads are great, our transportation is poor, you can't get a bus for love nor money, the trains are sporadic. Our high streets ebb and flow depending on how wealthy people are at the time. Pembrokeshire is not a wealthy area and is quite an elderly area, and so when I was asked if I'd get involved and try and fight the "Designed to Deliver Programme", I said, absolutely, yes I would. So, when the local Conservative Party came knocking and said, "Would you consider standing for us at the next Assembly elections?" it wasn't much of a thought process, I kind of thought inside, immediately, "Oh, I can do this. I can try and make a difference."'

CATHERINE THOMAS

Before becoming an Assembly member, from 1997, Catherine worked for Julie Morgan, the MP for Cardiff North, as Office Manager and Political Aide:

'I had thought, at one time, of standing for Cardiff Council and then I thought, no, I'm not ready yet. I was always somebody who thought you need to serve some sort of apprenticeship and I was enjoying working for Julie [Morgan] enormously. Then the next thing that came round were the second Assembly elections. I hadn't really thought about it, and I didn't have any grand plan at all. I didn't want to stand during the first elections. I was very happy to support friends who were standing and to do everything I could to enable them. But sometimes you get the "light bulb moment", something clicks, and when the second Assembly elections came, I thought, yes. They were looking for a candidate in Llanelli. It just felt right, and Julie was hugely encouraging and supportive and I decided that I wanted to go for it. It was the privilege of representing my home constituency, because I didn't want to stand for anywhere else, that never entered my head and, as I said, I hadn't planned any of it. It was just one day when I thought, yes, this feels right now, I am going to stand. But the only place I would have entertained was the Llanelli constituency, and I always make a point of saying "the Llanelli constituency" because it is not just Llanelli town – it goes to the Gwendraeth, Burry Port, Pembrey and Hendy, not just Llanelli.'

DAWN BOWDEN

'The election night was quite amazing. Even though in Labour Party terms, Merthyr Tydfil and Rhymney were seen as a safe seat, I never took that for granted. No candidate will ever tell you they believe their seat is safe. The constituency here campaigns as though this is a marginal seat, they will campaign for every vote. But I always felt that I was going to be the first candidate to lose Merthyr Tydfil and Rhymney for the Labour Party, because that's what all candidates feel. Candidates never think they are going to win. And I remember being at the count and I didn't want to go to the tables and look at the votes being counted and see what was happening. And, as we were getting towards the end of the evening, my agent came over to me and he said, "Come with me." And he took my arm, and he walked me around the tables, and all these huge piles of votes – he said, "That's all your votes, all in those piles there." For the first time I started to think we were going to win, and it was fantastic. But the thing that made me so proud that evening, more than the support that I had from the people of Merthyr Tydfil and Rhymney – which was incredible because they didn't know me, they put their trust in me, and for that I'm hugely honoured, and I feel so privileged to be in the Senedd representing them. But it struck me that I was the first woman ever to represent Merthyr Tydfil and Rhymney. In a hundred years of Labour representation in Merthyr Tydfil and Rhymney, starting with Keir Hardie in 1900, I was the first women to be elected. And that hit me as quite an historic moment and that made me feel incredibly proud. Whatever happens from here on in, the history books will always record that I was the first woman to represent Merthyr Tydfil and Rhymney. The first woman to have been elected in a hundred years of women's suffrage, and more than a hundred years of Labour Party politics in this town."

* * *

Chapter Four

THE SELECTION PROCESS:

Twinning, Top of the List, All-Women Shortlists, Zipping and Selection on Merit

The National Assembly for Wales in 1999 was a completely new body and, as such, there was a desire to ensure that it contained a balanced number of male and female members. In the first elections, and in subsequent ones, Welsh Labour and Plaid Cymru adopted positive action to bring this about, namely Twinning and Top of the List. The Welsh Liberal Democrats briefly considered a process of Zipping, while the Welsh Conservatives adhered to their process of selecting on merit.

WELSH LABOUR: TWINNING AND ALL-WOMEN SHORTLISTS

Labour's Twinning policy meant that constituencies were paired and would choose a male and female candidate, with the constituencies deciding between themselves which candidate was selected to stand. The party also adopted All-Women Shortlists, with the result that the party has been the most gender-balanced in the organisation and has gone even further in subsequent years. At the time of writing, of the thirty Labour Senedd Members, seventeen are women compared to thirteen men.

JANE DAVIDSON

'Well, it was a fairly unexpected experience. The process in the Labour Party, which I very strongly endorsed, was the recognition that, in the whole history of Parliament, until 1997, there had only ever been four women MPs in Wales, which was just ludicrous. And the Labour party therefore decided that they wanted to develop a new range of opportunities to enable women's representation. And the new National Assembly for Wales gave them the first major opportunity to deliver on that new representation. So, they did what was called a Twinning process. They asked the forty constituencies of Wales to band themselves together into twenty pairs of twins. Each of the twinned pairs was asked to select a man and a woman candidate, and those candidates were then allocated to one of the two constituencies, which meant that going into the election, the very first election for the National Assembly of Wales, there would be twenty male candidates and twenty female candidates in the constituencies. For Labour, which was largely a holder of constituencies, it was the most effective mechanism – literally overnight changing women's representation in politics in Wales. I must admit, I was incredibly proud of the Labour party for doing this.'

JULIE MORGAN

'I'm thrilled about All-Women Shortlists. I think it's one of the best things we've ever done in the Labour Party to get all those women there. There's no way I ever felt that it was because of lack of merit that we had so few women in politics. It was because everything was biased against them, and the party members, not consciously but unconsciously, saw the politician as the middle-aged man in a suit. That's how people see the politician, although we are shifting now, definitely. I was selected on an All-Women Shortlist and was very proud of it, and all the people who were against it said, "Oh, you won't be treated the same as everybody else, you'll be seen as a second-class citizen, because you had help to get here because it was an All-Women Shortlist." But after five minutes, nobody even thought about whether you were on an All-Women Shortlist or not. So, I've campaigned ever since to try to increase the number of All-Women Shortlists. Then I was very heavily involved, one of the leaders, of the campaign to have Twinning in the Assembly. As a new body, we wanted to have somewhere as open, as transparent as we possibly could have it, and we wanted representatives from all different lives, and obviously women were one of the main considerations at that time. So, I campaigned very strongly in the Labour Party for this Twinning arrangement, which meant we went in with equal numbers of men and women. There was a lot of resistance within the party. We had some great people who fought for it. Anita Gale, the General Secretary [of the Welsh Labour Party] led it from within the party. She was so determined. We sang outside Transport House, the Unite Building now – "We were Twinned to Win!" – and we won by a tiny percentage.'

TAMSIN DUNWOODY

'There was prejudice, certainly from men. I was told at the end of one selection process, "That's okay, you can go back and look after your pigs and your children now," which I thought was a bit patronising. But you certainly came across it quite frequently and certainly in the older communities, the older party membership would not be that keen on having a woman candidate, and I know a number of my colleagues did actually suffer direct discrimination.

Twinning, I think, was absolutely brilliant, really superb, a very proactive way to go forward in terms of creating equality within the Senedd [sic]. I think the problem with All-Women Shortlists was it created a lot more problems than it helped. There was a lot of resentment created because of it. People couldn't see why we needed All-Women Shortlists to actually try to balance the numbers of people coming forward, and the candidates, and making sure they were in winnable seats not just marginal ones.'

JULIE JAMES

'Swansea West was an All-Women Shortlist. It wasn't twinned with anything. The previous MP, Alan Williams, was very ill and had stood down, and there was a selection process for Swansea West. There was an argument in the party at the time because there was a chance that a male ethnic minority candidate in Swansea West would come forward and be selected. The party was very keen for somebody of a non-white background to be selected so they decided not to have an All-Women Shortlist in Swansea West for the MP selections in order to allow that to happen. When it came to the Assembly selection, of course, it reverted to being an All-Women Shortlist, as it should have been for the MP selection. A big range of candidates came forward and I was lucky enough to be selected. Even that was controversial because Andrew [Davies] stood down quite late in the process and so, instead of going through the normal ward selection one by one, they brought all the wards together in three rooms in the Swansea Guild Hall and they did like a "speed dating" thing, where all the candidates went around and had five-minutes of topic with each of the wards. And then each of the wards decided who to nominate at the end of that, which is a pretty unusual way of doing it. There were quite a few complaints, but I'm very well known in Swansea, so I got selected, I guess. Swansea West itself is a very progressive CLP

[Constituency Labour Party] and has no problem with All-Women Shortlists at all. It is interesting though that what's starting to happen is that All-Women Shortlists are for women and open shortlists are for men. And I think we've got to guard against that.'

VIKKI HOWELLS

'I'm not a fan of Twinning. I think All-Women Shortlists are more transparent and if you're going to try and encourage women into politics, I think an All-Women Shortlist is better than Twinning, just on a practical level. If you're working with a Twinning process, you need to work twice as hard because you've got to canvass two constituency parties instead of one. I myself, as a woman who was working full time and was a mother, found it really difficult to find the time to do that. And also, you're actually paying for any canvassing that you're doing, any literature you're sending out at that stage, you're paying for it yourself, so it costs twice as much as well. I think All-Women Shortlists are a great thing in the right place and at the right time. Welsh Labour at the moment is running with All-Women Shortlists across all seats across Wales, for Westminster, until we can get a 50:50 gender split. My personal view is that you should look at constituencies based upon their history of selecting women and if you've got a seat that's never selected a woman, either for Parliament or for the Assembly, then put an All-Women Shortlist in there. But where we're at, at the moment, there is a danger... I've got a lot of friends in the party who are male who feel that they are really excluded from the process. We've got a lot of talent that we are bypassing.'

JANE HUTT

'I was very involved in the Labour Party in looking at systems to get better representation of women, and that's where we came up with the Twinning campaign. That had to be two constituencies that agreed to select one man and one woman. That was very hotly contested, so we only just won that vote in a Labour Party conference. A lot of women, sadly some who are no longer with us, [were] involved in that campaign, [like] the late Val Feld, but we did succeed in winning the Twinning vote. This was '97 through to '98, we were fighting for this Twinning. It was only the Labour Party that was trying, and people weren't that interested in what we were doing. The 'Yes for Wales' campaign got the attention but there was much more concern about Twinning within the Labour Party. Some constituencies were very resistant, so people like Anita Gale, who was the General Secretary at the time, a lead woman who actually stuck with this all the way through [were important], and we did succeed. But we had to do a lot of campaigning within the party to get Twinning. Once it happened, it worked extremely well, because it was women competing with women, as well as with men. Fortunately, we did succeed in getting many of those women elected. Wales has been so male dominated in terms of elected representation. We got there, we got through, and the Assembly wouldn't be like it is now without Twinning. It was very important starting point to get a more representative Labour.'

LYNNE NEAGLE

'The Labour Party policy at the time was Twinning. Constituencies were twinned so that there would be gender balance in the First Assembly out of the Labour representatives. It was a very contentious policy at the time but I'm under no illusions that I wouldn't have been in the Senedd without it. So, Islwyn and Torfaen were put together as a pair of twinned constituencies. I had good links in Islwyn, with Labour Party Members there. I had some links in Torfaen, and I thought, "I'll put my name in here and see how I get on." I didn't honestly think it would come to anything; it didn't feel like a terribly realistic prospect initially. But I picked up a lot of nominations in Islwyn and then, for some reason, started to pick them up in Torfaen. I got shortlisted and then went to the hustings in both constituencies and won. A lot of people supported the policy in the Welsh Labour Party but there were a lot of people who were very disgruntled about it, because lots of constituencies had a "favoured son" who would have been seen as the natural person to take on that role. So, in all those constituencies where the seat was earmarked for a woman, there were inevitably disgruntled people. It wasn't the easiest selection process in the Islwyn constituency, where I had most of my contacts and had far more nominations. The man who was standing there was supported by a lot of people who really didn't like Twinning, so I felt that was pretty hostile, there were efforts to stop me getting on the shortlist for Islwyn, which they were successful at even though I had much more contact with people in Islwyn, but luckily, I got on the shortlist through the Torfaen constituency. There was a lot of animosity, especially around the Islwyn hustings – there was a row over the postal vote – but I remember it was a very hostile atmosphere. Once I was selected, obviously you crack on, you want to focus on winning the seat, and I did find some people were great with me, even people who'd opposed Twinning said, "Right, she's the candidate now, we just get behind her and back her." But there were some people who were unable to move on from that. It kind of developed, in a way, a sort of mythology about me, because people talked about, "Oh, she's been parachuted in!"'

JOYCE WATSON

'Jackie Lawrence in '95 was Leader of the Labour Group, [and] there was a proposal then by Anita Gale. She came along and asked if I would support All-Women Shortlists, and I said yes, I would definitely support it because at that point we'd only had four female MPs in Wales. Jackie Lawrence became an MP on an All-Women's Shortlist and, then of course, Anita Gale being Anita Gale, we ended up with seven female MPs in Wales as a consequence of that; huge strides of course out of forty. Fast forward to '99 – brand new establishment coming forward, and there was quite a number of us women who said, "We've got to do it now." And we did. We ended up with Twinning, where there were forty constituency seats, they were pared down to a pair of twenty, and there would be one man and one woman selected. Labour rightly thought that they would be the majority in the Assembly, or certainly be in a strong position, so that was the way to get women into government in Wales. That was it. It sounds simple but, no, it was not simple. It was the biggest row within the Labour Party that I have ever come across. But we got it through. We persuaded the Trade Unions. A lot of men didn't like what they were seeing, and a lot of women were being controlled, coerced, and told that it was unfair and believed it. And other women were afraid of going down this road because they thought that their status would be diminished, because they'd gone through on an All-Women's Shortlist. There were lots of different reasons for people being opposed to it, but what was absolutely the case for those people like me who supported it, we could see, history was telling us, it wasn't going to happen any other way. Then, of course, it was, "Where you going to get all these women from?" And this is the interesting thing, this is the point that always gets forgotten – to get on the list you had to first of all apply, whether you were a man or a woman made no difference, you had exactly the same application process, there was the same application form. Then you had an interview, just to see, and then you had the real interview to see what levels of knowledge you had, what you were going to bring as a person to the party and also more

43

widely to your constituents. Every man and woman went through that same interview process, every man and woman. Not once, not once to this day, have I ever heard anybody say to me, that that man had an advantage. Not once. But what I have heard, too many times to remember, that that woman had an advantage. And yet the status of going through all that process was identical.'

Plaid Cymru: Top of the List

Plaid Cymru's Top of the List approach was centred regionally, with the first name on each regional list being female. In 2003, the year of parity in the Assembly, the party stepped up their positive approach and, instead of alternating between male and female on the list, two women could head the list in target seats that were deemed to be winnable.

JOCELYN DAVIES

'Well, it would have been great if we didn't have to have a system. Both systems have problems attached to them. Usually, to get selected, you have a hustings. So, you get up and you make a tub-thumping speech, and everybody's clapping, and then you answer questions. When you actually do the job as a professional politician you very rarely have to do that. You're using a very old-fashioned method of seeing whether this person would be a good Assembly Member. It is nothing to do with whether you would be good in a team or if you are a strategic thinker, clever – it's your performance at making a speech, which is not the best way of picking representatives at all, and I think we need to think about how we select the winner, whatever system you have. With Twinning, there was a backlash in the party. Labour suffered the backlash from it. It wasn't accepted by local members and if you're going to twin a winnable seat with a non-winnable seat, which one is the woman going to go into? The top of the list? Well, if that's where you get most of your seats from, and for us at that time, that seemed the best way of getting women into the Assembly. So, it's not just having candidates, it's getting women into these institutions. And we could see from the first intake, and the second, I think, and perhaps the third, that those systems were working. But then, of course, after a little while you have people who say, "Well, we've done that now, we don't have to do it anymore, because we did it once." And it was okay when it was Jocelyn Davies, and it was Janet Davies, and it was Helen Mary. But who are these other people, these new people that we don't know, that they haven't got a track record? They are jumping over the heads of the "Dai Lloyds" of this world. I don't know what the answer is, but I know we can't give up on it just because it is not popular.'

JANET DAVIES

'In the '80s and '90s, Plaid Cymru was very enthusiastic about having women candidates for Westminster, and very happy having them doing so, but only in seats they couldn't possibly win. And for me, the big issue was not so much getting 50 per cent of the women candidates as getting 50 per cent of women candidates in seats that were winnable. And that's where we came up against real problems in the party. And of course, it really became stark when the Assembly came along, and we wanted to make sure there were quite a number of women elected to the Assembly. I was Director of Elections from 1996 to 2001, so a lot of responsibility was on me, and Helen Mary Jones, I think, was Director of Equalities, and we both worked together to try and actually deal with this. First of all, and for the first time ever, we set up a candidate register so that people were interviewed before they could go on the register. We strongly encouraged women to stand, to get on the register, we ran training schools. But at the end of the day, we still had to fight hard.'

JANET RYDER

'We took the decision, quite easily actually, that we knew we wanted our representation to be gender balanced. We had a pretty strong impression from the way information was going which constituency seats we would take, and we decided that we would pursue a gender balanced policy, but we wanted to make sure that the elected members represented that. It's very easy to have a gender balanced list of candidates but if you put the women in seats that are not going to get elected, you're not going to end up with a gender balanced proportion in the Assembly. So, we took the decision that we wanted that actual group to be gender balanced. As far as possible, we assessed what would happen. I can't remember what we did with constituencies, but I know women just were not getting elected in the seats where we knew we would stand a chance. It just wasn't happening, don't ask me why. It's women as much as men, because the constituency votes on it and there's as many women in Plaid Cymru as there are men, and they all vote on the candidate. So, it's a shift in female attitudes as well that you need to see, it's not just a male attitude. Some males are more pro-female candidates than women are. So, we decided that we'd look at the lists and we'd make sure that women were at the top of those lists. We balanced it, if you like, so that a lot of the women were on the lists. We did an awful lot in the local area. I worked an awful lot with Dafydd Wigley's wife, Elinor Bennett, to encourage women to put their names forward. In North Wales, we had some really high class, good quality women putting their names forward, but then when they weren't being selected, they were just dropping out. And who can blame them? These were top businesswomen, you know, we had some really good quality candidates who would have been fantastic in the Assembly, but they just weren't being elected. And what we decided to do with the lists was to have a male and a female list and you were voted for on where you stood on that list. So, the female list would always go first. If you were voted and you were top of the poll in the women's list, in your regional constituency, your name would go first. And then it was decided that a man's name would go in second, and then a woman, and they would do it like that all the way down the list.'

NERYS EVANS

'Before the election, obviously this policy [women at the top of the list] was in place when I got elected. But I started to work for the party [Plaid Cymru] in 2002, and within a month I was a member of the women's section and representing the section on the Executive Committee within three months. I believe the party was very proud of the fact that there was parity among men and women in the second Assembly. This happened because of positive differentiating measures, and we held detailed discussions internally about which measures it was necessary to continue with and I was part of, and led, some of these campaigns with other members, male and female in the party. So, I think it's very important that this policy is in place. I remember – after the election, and before the 2007 election, so after the nominations and when people had been chosen – fierce arguments and people leaving the party because of these decisions, people who hadn't been put at the top of the list, perhaps. But, at the end of the day, it isn't a matter of personalities but a matter of achieving parity. I think it is a shame that there have been changes. We are proud of the fact that there has been equality in the Assembly, and that has happened because of the mechanisms adopted by the Labour Party and Plaid Cymru, there's no two ways about that. But we have taken a step backwards because of the policy changes that have been made.'

Welsh Liberal Democrats: Zipping

The Welsh Liberal Democrats briefly discussed a positive measure known as Zipping, where it would be man-woman-man-woman all the way down the list, but this was never fully implemented or successful. The party rejected proposals for All-Women Shortlists for target seats, although former leader, Kirsty Williams, spoke up in favour of All-Women Shortlists. At the present time, ironically, the only LibDem member in the Senedd is a woman.

VERONICA GERMAN

'We had put forward a policy of "Zipping" for the list, because we knew that really it was the list where we were going to make the most gains. So, the idea was that you'd have woman-man-woman-man, so that across the regions you would have either a man or a woman and you would "zip" down. That had been put forward at this conference and then all these men were up there saying how unfair it was. Not only that but they were inarticulate in their arguments! The decision wasn't made. It was then brought back to a special conference after that, in Builth, in the showground. At that point, there was me and there was Kirsty [Williams] – and that's when I became friends with Kirsty – and one man spoke in favour. There was just us and it was defeated. We were devasted. It was a big disappointment. It could have been, in my list, that there was a man at the top, so it wouldn't have made any difference, but it was just the principle. I remember them saying, "Well, it'll be the best person for the job." I took the numbers from Parliament at the time and there were however many more men to one woman, and I said, "Are you telling me that means that men are – say it was fourteen – fourteen times better than women? Because that's what you're saying." But, no, I'm afraid the argument did not get accepted. But the good thing was that I hadn't really had too much to do with Kirsty before then, and we really got on, and we did a lot together then in the run up to the Assembly the next year.'

Welsh Conservatives: Selection on Merit

The Welsh Conservatives continued to select candidates on merit, regardless of gender, and female representatives were few in number, and remain so. Of the Conservative members serving in 2022, thirteen are male and only three are female.

LISA FRANCIS

'The members from each association – and there are, I think, nine of them, nine constituencies, then – all have a vote. There were two regional hustings, one in Carmarthen and another one in Rhayader where you got a chance to speak for ten minutes, and then take questions for ten minutes, and your CV was circulated. There was a postal ballot and so every member then made a decision. I was lucky to get that third slot because I wasn't very well known. I had some good advice from the likes of Nick Bourne who said to me, "You need to get yourself around every coffee morning, every fête, every village show that's going and get to know people." So, I did. I made sure that I was well known everywhere. I also made sure that my CV stood out – it stood out anyway because I think I was the only woman at that time who applied for the list. I realised I needed something to make me stand out, so I spent quite a lot of money on getting my CV absolutely right, my own money, and I think it paid off. That's really the only thing that a member has to go on. And I knew that if I was able to achieve that third on the list position, there was a chance that I might be elected. And the vagaries of the election system that we have, such as it is, meant that I was. That changed later on, in 2007. Angela Burns won the seat of Carmarthen West and South Pembs, and that made a difference, because the compensatory part of the voting system means that the list votes then go down or are taken away. I used to describe myself as a sort of "tail-end Charlie" – the rear gunner in a Lancaster Bomber, they were the ones most likely to "cop-it." So, I always felt that, as quickly as I was in, I would be out at the next election. And I tried to get higher up the list, but to no avail, sadly.'

LAURA ANNE JONES

Laura feels that she and Lisa Francis got to the Senedd on merit, rather than through any form of positive action, such as the measures employed by Welsh Labour and Plaid Cymru:

'Richard John in Monmouthshire County Council has now put a motion forward saying the aim is to get this Council 50:50 [men and women], let's make positive steps to make that happen, and I am all for that. I don't know how they're going to try and achieve that. I think they're going to do it in a more natural way than just All-Women lists, but just trying to find women candidates and encouraging them to step forward. I don't know what the answer is, to be honest, because you want it to be fair but, at the same time, it has to be the best person for the job. But we need women to get into that, and I don't know what the problem [is] with people selecting women. There seems still to be a preference for a man over a woman regardless of how good they are. We had some incredible women candidates in the last Senedd election, and it was a real shame that a lot of them didn't get into the Senedd. They would have been incredible. And they will be in the future: I know they'll get there, but it's just getting them there. Fairness-wise, you can see the reasons for it [Twinning]. We need to do something to make it happen but, at the same time, I don't want men to lose out because they are men, because how is that any better? It's a real struggle about how we do it. I'd love to do it naturally but we're having problems with that, so something needs to happen. Because we've exhausted that process [natural selection] first, maybe we do now need to start taking more action, and maybe more positive discrimination. Because even though I was dead against that, we've tried to do it the natural way. So, I'm open to ideas. I wouldn't say I'm dead against anything like that [positive action] but I do think we need to debate it and debate it honestly as a party.'

* * *

Chapter Five

PARITY: 2003 AND BEYOND

In 2003, the National Assembly for Wales became the first legislature in the world to achieve 50:50 gender balance between its female and male members, something Westminster has never achieved in its entire history. Thirty women were returned, winning half the sixty Welsh seats. In the thirty-strong Labour Group, there were actually more female members than male, with nineteen women elected compared to eleven men.

This significant and historic achievement was due largely to the positive efforts of Welsh Labour and Plaid Cymru, both parties using measures to ensure that female candidates were given priority and encouraged to stand for office, as we've seen in the previous chapter. The breakthrough of the "glass ceiling" in Welsh politics made world headlines and was hailed by women's rights groups both in the UK and across the globe.

Several of the AMs/MSs who were elected to this remarkable Assembly of 2003, and to subsequent Assemblies, were interviewed and asked how it felt to be part of that, how the legacy of it affected them, and also about the reasons why that parity has never been achieved since.

LISA FRANCIS

'I didn't really recognise at the time how important it was. I had always believed that I wanted to be selected and elected on my own merits, my own ability, not because I was a woman. Labour had a very strong positive discrimination policy going on, so a lot of the Labour women Assembly Members had been elected because they'd been placed in constituencies, and that comes with its own problems. I had strong views that constituency associations know what they want and should decide what they want. For me it was more important to have been chosen for my abilities. I remember my colleague Laura [Anne] Jones giving an interview and overhearing her saying to somebody, "Well, Lisa Francis and I have been selected and elected on merit, and that's the way it should be, it's quite different." And I remember thinking, "I don't really agree with that." I think we were very lucky to have been in the right place at the right time. And already I was starting to see the impact of having that 50:50 gender split. You can't just say, "Those people aren't entitled to be there because they weren't elected on merit," which is what it sounded like to me. Later on in that Assembly, it became very clear that, having that many women in, it was moulding the shape of it by the sorts of questions that were being asked, the work that was being done on committees, the way committees were doing their work, even. Women are more consensual by nature, they're more practical, in my view, they don't waste time. I know there are men who will argue about this, but this was my impression. And there was a very strong body of women in that Assembly, for sure, and they were very supportive and reached out to us, and that surprised me. I expected more "tribal lines" but I think women working together goes far beyond that really. There was an almost motherly concern of Labour Members like Rosemary Butler, Janice Gregory, and it would be almost like, "How are you getting on in your group, love, there's only two of you?" And it was great to have that support. And they would recognise if you were having an off day, or something had not gone well for you, they'd pick up on it, their sort of antennae, that female antennae that we have, would grasp that, whereas the men in your own group, it would happily pass them by. It could be a bit of a boys' club, because there just weren't enough women in our group. But it was very significant, looking back on it now, in the way it shaped the Assembly. So, I've gone full circle really, I've changed my opinion completely, now. I think positive discrimination is the way forward, it needs to happen, because it can't possibly be fair, can it, if we are over 50 per cent of the population, that we don't have that representation in our Senedd.'

LEANNE WOOD

'It's always the same with history, you look back and you see things are much more significant in retrospect than they ever felt at the time. I remember, it was great, you know. I would have phone calls from academics on the other side of the world – from Canada, from Australia – really interested in the fact that the National Assembly for Wales had achieved parity between men and women, and there were so few places that had come even close, and what did it feel like to be a part of this. And it almost got a bit boring to be doing these interviews because there were so many of them. Looking back now, what a great position that was, and I just don't think we even recognised at the time how significant it was, and we've only gone backwards since. It definitely did [raise the profile of Wales] because there was interest, TV crews would come to the Senedd [sic], and want to do interviews, students from everywhere, and especially if there were any kind of gender studies groups or any courses like that, yes, they took a keen interest. And that must have raised the profile, because people would have been writing articles and sharing that information whenever they returned to their home countries.'

CATHERINE THOMAS

'One of the first things that happened to me when I arrived at the Assembly was, I was walking around a corner and I literally bumped into three male Tory Assembly Members, who were sort of just giggling. I thought, "Oh gosh, is this what it is going to be like?" Because I'd won Llanelli, and it was so narrow, it wasn't expected, there'd been a feature in the *Western Mail* about me, and they were like little boys really, "Oh, we've seen you in the paper!" And I just thought, "Oh dear." And then, when I sat in that Chamber and I did look around and I saw the number of women, I was heartened. And I thought, "Wow!" Because again it was something that I'd been involved – along with many others – to campaign for. And then when you see the fruits of your labour in front of you and you are actually privileged to be part of it, and because you know the difference that it can and it will make, and it did and it does make, that is a very special feeling. And that's why I am passionate about continuing with positive action because you can't take your foot off the pedal. Because once you do, you slide right back, and it is needed. So, I was very much aware, and I felt honoured to be there. I was standing there in that photograph and just thinking, "Wow, this is a moment in history." And to be there, it was just wonderful.'

JANET RYDER

'Well, it shot Wales up. At one time, Wales was the only legislature in the world to have an equally balanced representative body, so it certainly put Wales on an international stage for recognition. The Equal Opportunities Committee did a lot of work, and I don't know if that would have been there if there hadn't have been all those women in the Committee. And you did start to look at things probably more from a woman's point of view, which can be slightly different to a man's point of view, sometimes, just the abilities that women have. How do you make sure that you break that glass ceiling? Well, we obviously didn't do that because that is still there, unfortunately, to some extent, there's still a long way to go. Partly, it's encouraging women to come forward, so you need to give them a role model and say, "Look it can happen, this is what you can do, you can make a difference, the ability is there for you to come through." It's supporting them when they come through into candidacies, it's making sure that all the political parties are signed up to it as well, or as much as possible, so that you get a good balanced representation across all political parties. What perhaps didn't happen, which may have helped, you possibly needed to form some sort of caucus group of women across the parties. And a lot of those women that were elected, especially in '99, they'd have been the women who were of that group, who'd been working for that, the Jane Hutts and the Sue Essexes, Helen Mary, you know, they sort of knew each other. But you needed to bring on another generation of women. If you look at other parliaments, in some cases there are parliaments where women across party can come together and discuss matters. And I didn't really see that happening within the Assembly and I think that would have been good, beneficial in some cases. It's always good to talk to people from other parties because you can get a much better consensus then when you bring legislation forward, and I think that was a shot that was missed.'

LYNNE NEAGLE

'I think at that time the fact there were more women in the Labour Group than men was very much a cause for celebration. The fact that the Senedd [sic] was meant to be a different kind of place was very much set out from the start really. We went in there knowing that this was an institution that we were hoping would be very different from Westminster. Obviously, I had a lot of women around me, with a lot more experience than me. I've always recognised that I wouldn't have got where I've got, to be a member of the Senedd, without the Labour Party taking that action on Twinning and being willing to have those fights. I suppose, because I was so much younger than some of the other women, and some of the women in the Senedd [sic], people like Val Feld and Jane Hutt, had years of experience campaigning on equality issues, so I was very much, I suppose, in their shadow. I have tried to do my campaigning on these issues more locally, in terms of trying to support women locally, arguing for quotas locally, because the battles weren't won. And I had an ongoing battle with some in the Labour Party for my presence there, really, an ongoing challenge that I feel I had to wrestle with for a long time. There was always a lot of commentary about the fact that we had so many women in the Assembly then and, I think, generally, we had very, very active women [which] meant that the profile continued to be high, so it definitely has made a big difference. Even just in the way the Assembly was initially set up, with the National Advisory Group and everything, putting in place things that would make it easier for women, although some of those have been rolled back on now.'

SIÂN GWENLLIAN

'I'm sure it has affected the culture. It had made the culture less quarrelsome, perhaps, compared with Westminster – that's where you think of arguments, and so on. It's really interesting. When we are discussing burning issues such as Brexit, and so on, very few women participate in those discussions – and they can get very contentious. I think, as regards creating a culture, that it's more compatible, somehow, which people want to see politicians do, talking sensibly and not shouting at each other. I think the presence of half of us being women has contributed to that. I also think regarding the issues we discuss... Evidence has shown, hasn't it, the more women who are in a room, more attention is given to topics that can affect women in general, that is, matters like childcare and so on. I think research has been done which shows that [in] the National Assembly, topics such as childcare and job sharing, and so on, have more attention here than they do in institutions where you have less of that equality. Having more women means that the lives of all women will be improved because we draw attention to the important things in our lives.'

DELYTH JEWELL

'Parity between the sexes is really important to me. It is disappointing in the Senedd that we've stepped backwards, in a way, because it used to be a 50:50 split, and now it isn't so much. We should find a way to get more women into the political world. There are specific challenges for women, because they are women – not that challenges aren't there for men, and they can be really difficult challenges – but the challenges that face women are often, unfortunately, because they *are* women, that's what makes it different. In spite of that, it is necessary to have women in the political world, because we bring something to legislating that is different. We bring different perspectives in, a different way of doing things, perhaps we're not quite so gung-ho all the time, but we find quite conciliatory ways of doing things. This is important to me and something I would like to do more of. The Senedd has been to the forefront in the world by ensuring parity between the sexes. But yet it shows that we can't take something like this for granted because we have slipped back. So many people can't understand why I work for women's rights, or who don't see that there is a need to be a feminist, who think the debate has been won. Of course, many of the arguments have been won, but we can't rest on our laurels, we can't take for granted that things are going to stay won. We must carry on fighting, we must get more awareness, because women have achieved a great deal within the devolved system, but there is a distance to go yet.'

ELIN JONES

'I think, in hindsight, we were guilty of not fully understanding the huge significance of the change which had occurred in the 1999 and 2003 elections. Seven women Parliamentary Members had been elected to Westminster from Wales, over 90 years – only seven. And very suddenly, over twenty women were elected to Wales's public political life in 1999. Therefore, there was a very substantial transformation in the number of women who appeared on television screens talking about politics, as well as how they influenced politics. I never saw myself as someone who needed to highlight this in any way. Because I was younger, I didn't know any better. Perhaps I hadn't had to fight as much as some who were older – Jane Hutt, Sue Essex, the Janet Daviesies of this world – who had been fighting within their parties through the years to get more attention for women. Thinking of the fact that, in 2003, we had the first ever democratic legislative Senedd [sic] in the world, to have elected a Senedd [sic] where men and women were exactly equal, and we didn't boast about it at all, we almost didn't celebrate that we'd done it, and we've almost forgotten to mention it. And, so, it is important that we think about how this is recorded and how to ensure that people in Wales remember that we were the first to break through what was, to all purposes, a glass ceiling. And by today, as I do this interview, we are 47 per cent of women. So, some say we are falling backwards but we haven't fallen as much as all that, we are still quite equal here. I don't think we made enough of it. We should have boasted about it more and we should have sent some of the women across the whole world, to try to influence and show what was possible in other places. We didn't fully see the enormity of what we had achieved in Wales. We mustn't forget how pioneering we were back then, and that mainly because of the steps two political parties, and especially the Labour Party, had taken to ensure that would happen. It hadn't happened without some hard work in the two parties, Plaid Cymru and the Labour Party, and especially the steps the Labour Party had taken in choosing women to stand in elections – Twinning.'

RHIANON PASSMORE

'What would I say, now, is I think the chamber is much more discursive, it's much more debating, and I for one don't believe women are just the quiet, soft ones. I actually think women are feisty and want to get to the heart of the debate. So, I don't actually believe that women are going to give you a softly-softly approach. It may have a different effect, a different impact, because we have different experiences, but I think that we've now got a more discursive approach in the Assembly [sic], and there is much more intervention and more heated debate. Some don't like it. Some say that it's not consensual politics, we need to be different to Westminster. Well, we are different to Westminster, but I don't think we should be different for different's sake. And I think it's important that, where we disagree, we are telling people that we disagree. I think it's a lie to the public to pretend that we all consensually get on; we don't. In terms of looking at the chamber and expecting everyone to be polite to each other, we expect politeness and the rules to be upheld, but there have been incidents when we've had really nasty stuff said, stuff that could be deemed to be out of order and *were* out of order. I would like to see things like that being treated very harshly in the Chamber. But I think just because there may be more women in that chamber, it does not mean that it's going to be more polite.'

JANE DAVIDSON

'Being a woman, being a feminist, being part of the women's movement, being immensely proud – not feeling I'd had any part to play in it other than being elected – but being immensely proud of being part of an institution that was making global history because of the representation of women. And being somebody who went out and talked about that a lot. I was particularly invited to universities and whenever I spoke about my role in education, I'd also point out that I was in the Cabinet which had this level of representation. And that was so important, as well, in putting over a message about the kind of new Wales, where equality was absolutely at the heart of the new Wales, where ambition was absolutely at the heart of the new Wales, and it would be a post-industrial playing to our strengths of a new Wales as well. It was part of the mantra that enabled me to be who I am everywhere because I had this immense backing that had been given to us by the people of Wales. It was the people of Wales who did it, not us. They elected more women than men, they elected many more Labour women than men. The trouble is, nowadays, when you look at it, without those measures in place we are in danger of this being a sort of historical blip and that some of the old habits in party selections are coming back.'

HELEN MARY JONES

'There is strong academic evidence that having that critical mass of women made a difference to what we discussed, it made a difference to the decisions we made. It also made a difference to *how* we discussed things. When you think, in the very early days of the Assembly, over the European Funding issue, we came to the conclusion that Alun Michael had to go and he was voted out. Now, if that had been done in the Westminster parliament, that would have been done with shouting and cheers and banging of desks. In the Assembly, it was done in total silence. And I think some of that was because we could see that that was a person, and we could see his distress, and his pain, and the sense that he had failed to do what his leader Tony Blair had asked him to do, which was to keep us all on a short leash. And we didn't. Now, you go into that place now and we see the banging of desks, and I don't like it. That's not the democracy I fought for. It's not the democracy my generation of women fought for. We were a phenomenon and we'd achieved that [parity] democratically. The disappointment for me was, you got to 2003, and both of the political parties had used affirmative action to get up to the point where the parliament was gender balanced. Me, and that generation of Labour women – people like Jane Hutt – we really hoped that then your role models would become more varied, and then when women began to put themselves forward for selection, without affirmative action, that it would become natural for women to be selected. Speaking for myself, I underestimated how ingrained that image is, when a Plaid Cymru member closes their eyes, and you say the word "politician" they're still seeing Dafydd Wigley and Gwynfor Evans. And so, we then saw that when the affirmative action programmes were, not entirely stopped, but kind of rolled back a bit, in both the parties, we began to drop back from 2007, and then into 2011 onwards. What was I thinking? That we could turn over four thousand years of patriarchy in fifteen years of democracy? No.'

* * *

Chapter Six

ASPIRATIONS AND EXPERIENCES

Women's Agenda, Sisterhood, Sexual Prejudice, Support

All the women we interviewed spoke on various aspects of women's agenda, ranging from the differing, or otherwise, aspirations and opportunities of men and women, sisterhood, within and across party, sexism and opposition that they faced, and the support they got from fellow female members, and from their parties and male colleagues too. Without exception, the women agreed that the Welsh Assembly/Senedd was more consensual because of the number of women present in the chamber, with a softer and less aggressive approach than that seen in Westminster.

Also, the tone of debate, as well as the subject matter of topics discussed, changed to include topics that might not have been raised or discussed if there hadn't been the number of women that there were – and still are – for example, in the arena of health care, the welfare of families and children, care for the elderly, equal pay, communities, etc. Several of our interviewees also spoke about sexism and opposition when they were standing for election, abuse on social media because they were women, and highlighted some of the inequalities that they faced from voters while out on the campaign trail.

JAYNE BRYANT

'Something happened when I was campaigning in the European elections, when Derek Vaughan was number one on the list, and he was already an MEP, but going again, and I was standing. Lots of people used to ask me what did my family think, what did my husband think? I wasn't married at the time. At first, I thought people were interested in who I was, but then I started to get people saying to me, "What does your husband think of you going to Brussels maybe?" And I started to think that nobody was ever asking Derek about his family background or what did his children think, it never ever came up. But for me, everywhere I went somebody would ask me about that. And I hadn't thought that I might be going away, and if I had children, what would I do with them. It was almost like they were trying to tell me something. Another one was when I was campaigning in the Assembly elections. I was really quite shocked when I knocked a door, and a man opened the door, and he said to me he wouldn't vote for me because he didn't know if I had children. I said I didn't have children and he said he's definitely not voting for me because he didn't know when I *intended* to have children, and on that basis, he couldn't possibly vote for me. I was so shocked. That was not the attitude I expected, and obviously that was only one person, but I was struck that somebody felt they could ask me that and that that would form the basis of their vote. That really shocked me that – in 2016 – that was an attitude. Nobody asks a man about his family background, but women often get asked those sorts of things.'

NERYS EVANS

'I have always campaigned for women's rights. It's integral to lots of women and, perhaps, we do it without thinking about it. I'm still a member of the women's section of Plaid Cymru. I think every woman MS in the party is a member, it depends how active you are, of course. There was a cross-party group on women in democracy in the Assembly. This was a closed group – usually they're open to the public – a place for the members of other parties to discuss the reality of being in the Assembly, the challenges, the problems, the tensions that arise in every party. Some of the stories I heard made you realise that Plaid Cymru was progressive, though they fought – are still fighting – internally to get equality. I remember Kirsty Williams going for the leadership of the [Liberal Democrat] party and being asked, "How will you juggle this with your three children?" I've never heard a man being interviewed in this way – has anyone asked Boris Johnson how many children he has and, secondly, how would he cope? This was a private forum to discuss the reality, on how to get that support, and to share tips, on how they managed processes, chose candidates, mentoring, and so on, and to help one another. One thing that struck me as different from being on the Assembly staff to being elected a politician, is that there were many more tensions between parties. I think that, when you have been elected an Assembly Member, you realise that you are in this weird group of people, that live a life between two places, representing people, up for scrutiny. And I think that tensions, the pressures, bring you together, regardless of party. Certainly, when I was there, there were cross-party friendships on these issues, and practical help available too. One of the things I was proud of, one of the advantages of having 50 per cent representation, was that issues were discussed, and campaigned on, and had notice, that you wouldn't necessarily have seen in Westminster and other places – the rights of carers, equal pay with men, etc.'

LESLEY GRIFFITHS

'I think people behave better sometimes when there are women around. Don't get me wrong, the women can be just as difficult as the men. For me, in the Chamber, I think I've rarely been called to order by the Presiding Officer. I can remember a couple of times, but if you don't feel passionate about it, you wouldn't be there. I remember shouting across the Chamber once and being told to stop shouting. Sometimes it is very frustrating when people can't see your point of view, but I always think that if you shout, then you've probably lost your argument a little bit. The Presiding Officers have never allowed it to degenerate in the way that we've seen in Westminster, and I think that's good, because how do you say to children and young people, "Look, you need to behave in a certain way, though it's okay when you're in the House of Commons you can behave in any way you want." So, I do like the fact we don't see that behaviour in a way that is seen in Westminster. I do remember one particular debate – it was between the First Minister and one of the opposition leaders – and thinking, "Oh, my goodness, this is going to really degenerate," and being quite taken aback and not liking it, in a way, and talking about it after to a couple of female colleagues who said they'd felt quite scared. I wouldn't say I felt scared, but it took me aback, because that's not the way we behave. I don't mind being heckled at all – you can heckle me all day long. And I think people like to see that passion, but I don't think people like to see bad behaviour. So, I do think people do in general, men in general, behave better if there are women present.'

ANGELA BURNS

'I think we may have a different way of achieving it, because I think that women are by nature far more inclusive, and by nature far more collegiate. We're much more, sort of, keen to get people to sit down and talk about things and make things happen. When

I was the only woman on the Welsh Conservative team, I was absolutely resolute, thinking of my background and where I'd been. I do remember I did have a conversation right at the very beginning and it was suggested to me that I might like to go off and do women and children, and social justice, or something like that. Now, women, children, and social justice are incredibly important, but I sure as hell was not going to be typecast into softer subjects, and away from business, finance, some of the tougher subjects. I felt very strongly that women sometimes do get typecast into those kinds of agendas. As I say, they're really important and, in fact, children is one of my big things, and I embrace it willingly, but at that time, I just thought, "No, I'm not going to be the token Tory, and the token Tory woman who does that sort of bit," and that's why I made a very strong play for chair of the Finance Committee after about a year, because Alun Cairns was the chair of that, and I was sitting on the committee and I made it very clear to Nick Bourne that I expected that I should be the chair of it because of my experience, rather than have a "bloke" come in and do it because I was "the woman."'

LISA FRANCIS

'Maybe men go in more with a "one thing" agenda. I think women, probably a bit more like me, embrace different things, see different things going on that they get interested in. Certainly, I think they're more interested in things that affect their families and communities – health, education. Men seem to be interested in things to do with finance, the economy. I'm not saying there are women who are not interested in that, but I think that's fashioned the sort of questions that are asked. In terms of where they see themselves going, I think the longer you serve, that changes, you see people grow in the subjects they are interested in. I think men go in with an idea of, "Where am I going to be in five years' time? I want to be a leader of my group, or I want to be Deputy Leader, or I want to be Chair of whatever, I want this certain portfolio." I don't think women are conditioned to do that so much. I think that's a problem because we tend to hang back. Maybe it's changed with the people who are in the Assembly [sic] now. But my generation, I think we were a bit, you know, you wait till you're asked to do something. Although I changed in that respect. I actually asked for something. I was on the Economic Development Committee. Two from our group were allowed to be on that Committee, and Labour decided that we should only have one member. And of course, that was vitally important for me because that committee included tourism. Alun Cairns was the other person on that committee with me and he was the main spokesperson. And Nick [Bourne] said, "I've got to take you off that committee, because that's the rules now." I was mortified, [and said], "Who's going to speak for tourism? He [Alun] won't have the same passion or commitment as me." He probably would have but I was really horrified that I was going to be taken off this committee. But by that time, I'd got confident enough to say, "Well, actually I'm going to ask for something else," because if you take something away then you've got to replace it. I think I became very difficult. I went to see Nick and said, "I'm not accepting this. You've got to get me back on that committee. I'm not having it." Completely unrealistic, it was totally out of his hands. He then offered me business manager. I think he thought, "Well, she really wants to get her teeth into something." And boy, was that something to get your teeth into! It taught me to be bolder and braver, and I'd like to think that the women who are there now have that mindset rather than taking what you're given and just settling for that.'

RHIANON PASSMORE

'I was Chair of the Welsh Women's Policy Forum for Labour, Chair of the Welsh Women's Committee, very much involved in the Political Parties Act in terms of that campaign, and I really wanted and understood the importance of women in politics. In regard to my current work now within the Commonwealth Parliamentary Association, I am the executive member with the British, Ireland, and Mediterranean Region Women's Steering Committee, where we're looking at gender issues across the small nations, and we've just put together a new strategy in that regard. I've just come back from the Falkland Islands, before Covid, and it's only when you see other legislatures, when you're privileged enough to see them, to see how they work, to see the gender balance or lack of gender balance, to see how women are treated, or not treated in an appropriate manner, as they should be, that you realise that we are way ahead of the game. I feel that by looking at what others are doing and helping in those regards, in terms of what those legislatures are doing, it's really important that we make sure there are the facilities, there is the support, that there is the understanding, and there is that context of what extra women in the majority do.'

JANE DAVIDSON

'I think sisterhood is really important. I remember the first person who ever said to me about Margaret Thatcher not being in sisterhood, it was like something clicking into place, and I realised what was wrong. That there were women who pulled the ladders up after them and there were women who dropped the ladders down. And I think there was a real feeling of sisterhood [in the Assembly]. I don't think there were any Conservative women in the first administration or if there were it was only one, but there was very much a sisterhood between the other parties. It was helped by the fact that I knew one of the Liberal Democrat Representatives, Jenny Randerson, because we'd been on the City Council together. I knew Helen Mary Jones because of her campaigning on equalities, for example, and Kirsty Williams who came in as a new Assembly Member and went through all her pregnancies in the Assembly, so was seen very much as the next generation. There was a sisterhood amongst the older Assembly Members and there was a sort of support for younger Assembly Members. And I think that sisterhood was really important. It wasn't so much for me about *friends* across party lines, as *respect* across the party lines, and knowing that there were some elements we'd all go to – all those of us who were very strongly supportive of the representation of women in the National Assembly. We'd go to the meetings, we'd go to the celebrations, we'd take part in initiatives around International Women's Day. Rosemary Butler convened a dinner for years linked to International Women's Day that we all went to year after year. It was really nice knowing that you had that level of comfort and support and knowing actually that you could have gone to any of those women at any point on any issue related to gender and have confidential conversations. So, it was a very different atmosphere dealing from women to women. I know that, and particularly in the Labour group, some of the more traditional men – when it was seventeen women and thirteen men – found it very threatening that that was the case and would talk about us "ganging up" on them. Oddly enough we were ganging up in terms of trying to create kinder politics, so I think I was in the right gang!'

VIKKI HOWELLS

'There is a feeling of sisterhood, definitely, but [I] wouldn't say that it transcends everything. I think that age is an issue, as well, so some of the younger Assembly Members may feel they've got more in common with each other regardless of gender and regardless of party. There is definitely a strong feeling of sisterhood and a good example of that would be the campaign for purple plaques, that we established, and that had cross-party support. I like to think of myself as being post post-feminist, but it can raise some eyebrows when you say that. Perhaps that's just due to my own walk through life – that I've never felt that my gender has held me back, but I'm well aware that there are many other people who would feel different to that. That comes to the fore when you feel that somebody is struggling or fighting back against a system, and particularly in relation to the way that Assembly Members are treated on social media. That's where I think I've seen women from all parties really coming together to support each other because of the torrent of abuse that you can face on social media. And I do think that that is an issue that is predominantly driven by misogyny.'

JANET DAVIES

'I found that differences within women's groups and within the men's groups were probably bigger on the whole. Most women want to see a good society, with equal opportunities, good education, good health care, and quite a lot of the men do as well. I think where I saw the split was between, particularly, some of the men in the Conservative group, where they didn't seem to have that view at all. Not everyone, but there was some of them who were clearly thinking more about their career in life and what they could do to get a high profile and get elected to Westminster rather than what they could do for Wales. And I think I saw that as a bigger gulf than, say, a gulf between me and one of the Labour men who was a minister. Perhaps because there *were* so many women there, the gender issue seemed to be of a lower profile.'

JULIE JAMES

'You hear a lot of stuff about how hard it is to be a woman politician, and all the abuse you get on social media, that sort of stuff. And to some extent that's true, there is a fair amount of nonsense that goes on, on social media, and I think that's probably worse the younger you are. The more established a person in your own right you are, the more resilient you are to that kind of thing.

I can entirely see that if I'd been twenty-six and not fifty-three that I might have been much more affected by that kind of name throwing and so on. But what you never see is the plus side. You never see the fact that you have a real chance to change the way that things are for people and to influence the way that we live our lives. And the fact that the Assembly [sic] has so many women in it means that priority is given to things that matter in a way that hasn't been seen before. It's been interesting with Covid-19 that we've been able to emphasis the resumption of childcare and informal arrangements of that sort as being absolutely essential to the economy, whereas that didn't happen in England. So, it's that kind of thing where you do have a major influence on the way things work in the country that you are representing. And in your local area, you haven't got any hard power, but you can get people into the room, you can get them to talk to each other, you can get them to see each other's point of view, you can move things forward in that kind of consensual way that I think suits a lot of women in terms of the way they work anyway. And the other thing I emphasised all the time is that, behind the scenes in the Senedd, with the exception of the minority parties that were elected in the last election, almost everything we do is consensual, even with the Conservatives. Because politics in Wales is actually quite a lot left of centre than where it is in England, and that's because we have a soft influence on the political discourse of the country.'

JENNY RATHBONE

'I think close friendships with women in other parties, not so much. I just think we are all extremely busy, and we don't see that much of each other really. But certainly, I've always endeavoured to find consensus on things we can agree on because that is one of the ways in which you get change. So, I've always collaborated with whoever wants to collaborate with me. And certainly, in this fifth term, I feel there has been a step change in our ability to organise. I chair the Women's Health cross-party group and I think we've achieved some important things around improving the way in which medical abortions are delivered, and that's been particularly important during the lockdown. And raising women's health concerns, ensuring that women have a voice. Things like endometriosis is something that is suffered by one in ten women. It's not something that gets talked about very much, whereas the cancer lobby is very well organised. I've been a feminist activist since the early 1970s, so women's role in the world is very important. I think it's enabled us to point out, for example, that, of the chairs of committees that are held by the members of the Labour Group, they are predominantly men. And we need to make more effort to ensure that we have a balance of people, of both men and women. So, I think these things are really important. I think that we haven't won that fight yet. We have to keep going on it. And occasionally men need reminding. Some of them fall into old ways occasionally. It's all done in a camaraderie way, but we don't have a perfect society, yet. So, we need to keep women's issues, children's issues. I think women are much more likely to fight for children than men.'

LAURA ANNE JONES

'I've got lots of friends cross-party. I was just talking to Delyth Jewell – who's obviously a South Wales East Plaid Cymru member – last night. Of course, we don't agree with everything that comes out of each other's mouths when it comes to proper policy, but when it comes to the good of South Wales East, we'll work together on a lot of things, and I love that constructive approach. It's important that we "big each other up" as well and that does happen cross-party, though some women in the Labour Party don't, but a lot of them do, a lot of them do in Plaid Cymru as well. As a rule, the women are very supportive of each other, and helping each other, and I love that, I feel a real sense of that. But particularly in our party, led by the wonderful Suzy Davies, I think that women have really come together. We've got our own WhatsApp group, where we talk about the women's side of stuff and how best to support each other in canvassing or standing for this, that and the other, and when someone's got a position in the Council, or something in our group, it's, "Well done, that's brilliant," or doing a speech, people will support them. It's just really a lovely community at the moment and that's changed massively in the last twenty years for me. To have that now, I think we're in a really good place in the Conservative Party. The women's side of the party is really strong, such talent, really good people coming forward and paving the way for others. We're in a good place, we just need to get them selected in the key seats now, that's the next step. As a party, we are attracting really good women into it, and to it, so that's a good sign, that our policies are attracting the right people. So, really positive and always so supportive of each other and I am proud to be a Conservative for that reason at the moment. When I was first elected, it was very few and far between, and actually the women were telling me that I should go off and have children – "You shouldn't be having a career, you should be having children, settle down and let the man to do the work..." – that craziness I had to fight against. But I don't feel like I have to fight against that anymore, which is really nice.'

* * *

Chapter Seven

A FAMILY-FRIENDLY INSTITUTION?

In 1999, when the Assembly was established, there was a strong desire to ensure it was a much more 'family-friendly' institution than Westminster, and there was an effort to establish family-friendly working hours, which were written into the formal Standing Orders. The presence and input of so many female members were at the root of this desire and plans were laid down for a crèche, for childcare, for more normal hours – if not exactly nine to five, flexibility around sittings that allowed parents – men and well as women – to collect children from school, women on maternity leave and with young babies, etc.

As the first term progressed, however, it became clear that the weight of work involved in being an elected politician wasn't always compatible with family life, especially around times of late-night voting in the chamber, surgeries, meetings and other activities in the constituencies at weekends and evenings, and for those members not living in Cardiff, the long distances travelling and spending time away from their homes, partners and children. However, everyone we interviewed agreed it was streets ahead of Westminster in this respect and also that the desire and effort to make the Senedd more family-friendly is still there within the institution.

CHRIS CHAPMAN

'We started off with this idea that it was going to be a family-friendly Assembly in terms of the hours. It wasn't great. The committees should start at, say, half-past eight, nine o'clock and the proceedings should finish at half-past five. But I think that's all gone by the board, now. It was quite difficult to keep those arrangements because there was so much packed into the Assembly proceedings and sometimes the sittings are quite late sittings, though not as late as Westminster. There was talk in the early days of having a crèche, etc, but I don't think that happened, and whether that would have worked anyway, for people who lived away. There's always been a challenge about it being family-friendly but there was a genuine attempt to make it work. When they set up the Assembly, they wanted to enshrine these principles into it. My children were teenage so obviously I didn't have to put them off to school or anything, I was of an age when it didn't trouble me, but I think if I'd been someone with a young baby, it would have been really challenging.'

LEANNE WOOD

'I had my daughter at the beginning of 2005, so I was a fairly new Assembly Member. But in terms of home, that was where all my support was. My partner didn't work and so was able to provide full time childcare, as well as run the house and allotment, and everything else. So that just freed me up to be able to do my job. It's difficult enough, I think, having a child and working full time – full stop. But to try and do that with the hours that politics demands, and being away on weekends, conferences far away from home, lots of overnight stays, I just don't see how it would have been possible if my partner had been working full time as well, or if I was a single parent. I just don't know how people are able to juggle things when they're in that position. I also live in the same street as my parents and so they've always been around to provide additional emergency childcare should it be needed. I've always had fantastic support at home, and I couldn't have contemplated running for the Plaid Cymru leadership had I not had that support there.'

VIKKI HOWELLS

'A lot of it comes down to your support network. I'm really lucky because I've got a strong family support network, but I also find the job is quite flexible, as well. My daughter, when I was first elected, was really taken aback by the fact that I could start to take her to school twice a week. I could pick her up from school twice a week. Working as a teacher, I'd never been able to do that. So, there are ways in which, as a politician, you can manage your workload around key things like picking up the children from school, doing some work from home, or if your constituency office is close to home, close to your child's school, nipping out to pick them up. And those things really do make all the difference. I know that the Senedd [sic], when it was established, was designed to be family-friendly and have more family-friendly working hours, and if you compare it to Westminster, there's no doubt about it, we are streets ahead. But on a Tuesday and a Wednesday, it can be difficult when you're not voting until quite late and you might not get home until nine o'clock at night, and if you wanted to stay for some of the evening events on issues that are important to you and your constituents.'

KIRSTY WILLIAMS

'When I first moved to the constituency, I lived in Builth Wells, because it was in the centre, but very quickly after my election, it became very clear to me that I could not commute every day from Builth Wells. And although the allowance system allowed the Assembly Member for Brecon and Radnorshire to have a flat in Cardiff, I did not want to stay in Cardiff, I wanted to get back. So, I moved to a small village just outside Brecon and I used to commute back and forth as much as possible. I was elected in May 1999, and I got married in September 2000, having promised him [her husband] it would be family-friendly working hours. I was the first Assembly Member to have a baby while elected, in 2001, when my daughter was born. I subsequently went on to have another daughter in 2004, and another daughter in 2006 – expertly planned in between elections! Has it been difficult? Ask any working mum who has tried to juggle a new family. I had a four-year-old, a two-year-old and a brand-new baby and this job. I went back to work three months after [the first], four months after [the second], and I had a little bit longer with [the third] because she was an April baby and that meant I caught the summer recess. Would I do that now? No, no I would not. It wasn't good for me, and I don't think it was good for them. The pressure to get back... and there was nobody to ask because nobody had done it. And I feel really strongly there should have been more support and more help. And I'm really glad that now, finally, when Bethan Sayed will have her child, there will be more support for Bethan. Because there was not support there for me, and there was not a great deal of support for Lynne Neagle, or for Leanne Wood, who have been the Assembly Members that have gone on to have children.'

NERYS EVANS

'I don't think you consider the implications and pressures on parents until you become a parent. Perhaps you think you do but, from the process I've been through over the last few years, becoming a parent, there is immense pressure, and in addition to that, for members from North Wales as regards travelling. I was always having this argument, when I was an AM, about family-friendly hours. It was an unpopular opinion, that I voiced at the time, that the hours the Assembly sat were only friendly if your family was in Cardiff, and if you could leave at five or six o'clock in order to be home with the family. But if you were a member with a family in West or North Wales, those parents – women and fathers – would have preferred to sit longer a couple of nights mid-week so that they could be home with their families. This argument went on a lot. But the Assembly has a proud tradition of being for and supportive of families. We saw Leanne Wood bringing her young daughter into the Chamber, it was a very proud moment for us all that she was able to do that, that it was open for her to do that. I think you have decisions like that, you have ethos like that, when women, and fathers, parents are in a position to make decisions about how the institution operates. I think this is a great advantage for us in Wales, since there are so many women, but also, it's clear that women do most of the caring in the home, of parents and children, and that's an important thing. So, we have seen the advantage of that in the Assembly, because so many women are in roles of power to make those decisions.'

JOCELYN DAVIES

'I think your family has to be very patient and as committed as you, because if they're not, then this is a stress. You're leaving very early in the morning, you're doing a lot of hours, you're coming home late. A lot of working people have the same problem, but I think – especially when I look at the Assembly now, when it starts to sit a bit later, and a bit later, when you can't be certain what time you're finishing at the end of the day – with young children, that must be incredibly stressful. Because there's very little support, in terms of physically in the building, if you've got a child, especially when the numbers are so narrow, so the Government Members *have* to be there. Certainly, from being a Whip, we did use to take into consideration if people needed to go. Your children are only young for a short period of time. You can't make up for it later. Just having family-friendly hours doesn't quite go far enough. I remember just being in the canteen and there was one highchair – not that I've ever seen a child in it – but that's not enough. You very rarely saw Assembly Members' children in the building. It's not welcoming in that respect. My partner was very patient and prepared to do it, and I had my parents who lived close to me who were prepared to do it. I'm from the valleys so there is family around, traditionally you can do it. But I'm sure that it has meant that people have not had as many children perhaps as they wanted to have, or that their partners have had to make bigger sacrifices than perhaps is acceptable today. If you're elected in North Wales, is your job in Cardiff? Well, not really, your job's in North Wales. You're representing the people of North Wales. We might find that since having to have virtual meetings during the Pandemic we might find that perhaps people don't always have to travel. I used to find it difficult if the recess was different from the school holidays, that can be difficult. And I know that the Assembly Members are well paid and can have childcare but being a parent is an important job as well. People are more sympathetic now with all sorts of jobs – people being able to have their work-life balance, because you're better at your job for it.'

BETHAN SAYED

Bethan Sayed, the Plaid Cymru Regional Member of the Assembly for thirteen years, in August 2020 announced her decision to step down from the Senedd to spend more time with her five-month-old son because politics wasn't family-friendly:

'Certainly, issues have been raised which perhaps haven't been raised at the Westminster level, because there are more women. For example, in my situation now, on maternity leave, I had to lobby to get someone to work while I'm away – I call him a "locum AS" – someone part-time. I had to appeal to the remittance board for this. And it's only now that they are thinking of re-introducing a crèche. They got rid of the crèche because not enough people were using it. So, though we say we're good, there are lots of things that still don't work for equality. There is a proxy system of voting now too – Dai Lloyd is voting on my behalf while I'm away. This didn't exist before either, until now. So, you only see changes sometimes through campaigning, rather than there being an institutional change to help equality. People say it is "family-friendly", but it isn't. You finish at the Senedd, say, at seven o'clock, which is better than Westminster, but then you go to an event someone has arranged, or you host something, or you go to the constituency to go to a public meeting or an event. There isn't a period when you just go in at ten and home at seven or half past seven. There's still a long way to go yet, I think. I want to be a politician but I'm finding it difficult, at the moment, to know what the right thing to do is. My life has been in politics since I was nineteen/twenty years old. I've been able to do everything during these times, but am I going to be able to balance my life and be a good mother too? I'm not sure yet because my husband owns a business, he's running around, working long hours, and at present I can be here as a sort of rock for the family. But if I'm elected again, and have to work seven days a week, how realistic is that? I'm very worried about this at the moment. That's the reality.

It isn't flexible enough at present, as Siân Gwenllian, Senedd Member for Wales, said, it would be good, perhaps, to have a two people system to share the role of the member. People haven't had agreement about this yet to put this idea forward, but perhaps I'd feel a little bit better going back if I knew there was someone doing it with me part-time. Obviously, someone with the same sort of principles as me, the same sort of beliefs, where I didn't feel I had to do everything.'

RHIANON PASSMORE

'I feel that we should have a nursery or a crèche within the Senedd and I cannot understand why we don't. So, we're working in that vein at this moment in time. I cannot imagine what it would be like - because I'm now a single parent -, I cannot imagine what it would be like if I had young children, no older support mechanism, and this crisis in terms of the workload that I've got. Therefore, systems have to come in, then, when this is the case. And we do have abilities within the Assembly, the Senedd, to bring in extra help, and I have had support from them in the past. I have to say, as a politician, I'm looking at this through two lenses. If you're coming in there with children – we obviously have lots of school groups and college groups, and I welcome them regularly – it's absolutely fantastic and you've got the facilities there. But if you don't have a crèche, and if you don't have a nursery, I can't answer that question [is the Assembly family-friendly?] without saying "no". And that's not to say people won't say, "If you need childcare, we'll arrange something for you." There are ways and means of doing that. But you will often find that parents don't want an *ad-hoc* babysitter to come from somewhere that they don't know about, they want something *in situ* that is trusted, that they've got a regular turnover of staff, and that there's an ability therefore to think right, that's over there, I can now go to speak as a witness in this committee.'

JANET RYDER

'There was an awful lot of work involved and I was in Cardiff a lot more than I wanted to be. To begin with, you're in a different hotel every week, and it was really difficult to settle anywhere. Over the summer, we bought a flat in the Bay, to have a settled place, and that meant as well that the family could come down occasionally, if I needed to stay in Cardiff at the weekends. So, it was tough. I think it was emphasised really on the big opening day, when the Queen came and officially opened the Assembly, because they split us up. We could go and sit beside our spouse in St David's Cathedral for the service, so that was fine. But then after that, they split us up and, as members, we were taken to the National Museum for a big meal and spouses were taken back down to the Assembly and given a big meal there. And we didn't see them again until just before the big concert in the evening. And most of the spouses were women. It wasn't family friendly. To get the group up and ready for anything in September, you virtually had to work through the summer, with interviews for staff, organisation, and things like that, I couldn't do that. I couldn't come home and do everything, like the cleaning and the cooking, anything like that, because you get home and you've got to pick up on all your constituency stuff. You've got this non-stop life, where you're in Cardiff and you're working on committee stuff, you're working on things like that, you're away from your family, especially from North Wales and Mid-Wales, you're away from your family, you don't get to see them. And when you get home, you can't just have a weekend off, because you only have Thursday, Friday, Saturday to pick up all the constituency stuff that's going on as well. You're out really long hours on those days as well. It didn't take into account, really, half-terms, and North and South Wales half-terms didn't always coordinate, so I sometimes didn't get a half-term break with the family. You were busy right through the summer recess.'

ELUNED PARROTT

'I was very lucky because my region includes the Assembly itself, so I was perfectly able to live at home and commute into work every day. It was very easy for me and relatively easy as well to maintain a work-life balance. I came home almost every night, but I was working very long hours, and you feel like you're torn in half, because you can never do enough as a mother. In our society, you can never do enough as a mother anyway, and there's always someone judging your choices. But I felt like I was never doing enough in the Assembly either. So, I was torn in half, I really was. I went through some periods of real stress where I just felt utterly inadequate and yet I was putting my heart and soul into things. Being an Assembly Member is a challenging thing. I remember always taking my phone with me on holiday, so you've got family holidays, and mum's on the beach with her phone out replying to just the urgent emails. I remember I'd just arrived in the Lake District, for a funeral, and just as I got out of the car, the phone went, and I was being asked to okay a press release. You have to accept that it isn't a job, it's a life, and if you have caring responsibilities, then doing that and being a politician is difficult. If you have a family, you have to have a support network around. Antoinette Sandbach, another Assembly Member from my era, who was a single parent, and she found it hugely challenging to juggle that. As a single parent living in North Wales, it's almost impossible to actually do the job. I think that we have a long way to go to make things possible for a wide range of people – and it doesn't matter if you're a man or a woman – if you're a single parent and you live in North Wales, but you're expected to be in Cardiff four days a week, how exactly are you going to do that? It just doesn't add up from that point of view. So, I think we need to make sure that we are thinking about those kinds of family circumstances.'

ANTOINETTE SANDBACH

'I pushed very much for an allowance for Assembly Members with young children. My daughter was nine when I was elected, which was an extremely young age for her to have to go away to school. Because I didn't have immediate close family living around me, it was absolutely impossible for me to have family support. And I argued very strongly at the time in the Assembly that the policies were not at all family-friendly for people in my situation. It was family-friendly if you lived near Cardiff, but it was a four-and-a-half-hour drive from North Wales to the Assembly. I don't think the support in the Assembly was nearly good enough for those with caring responsibilities, and I would say that's not just young children. We're a "sandwich generation" where many people are dealing with parents with dementia or other caring needs. If you genuinely want to support people to do the job, I think you have to pay them better so that people from any background can afford to be elected. It should be a scheme that is properly invoiced, if you have to arrange childcare, that's a legitimate cost. I know the argument is that there are lots of people working as nurses or doctors who have to look for their own childcare. There's no easy answer but it's a very practical problem and one that I think is a barrier to women going into politics, because it is normally the women who do the childcare. So, you risk getting either women who don't have children or older women whose children are much older and you potentially miss out on a sector of experience because you're not getting that "woman's voice" in the Welsh Assembly. I know certainly in Westminster there is an increased accommodation allowance but again that has an impact on how families work, because you can't have a child in school four days a week in Cardiff and one day a week in Llangernyw, and your surgery's done on a Friday. So, if you had accommodation in Cardiff, you could put your child into a school in Cardiff, and attend the Assembly, but there still needs to be someone that, when you're in the region doing your constituency work, can bring that child from Cardiff to the North on a Friday. That problem was never addressed.'

LYNNE NEAGLE

'In the beginning, we had "family-friendly" written into our Standing Orders, so we would have to finish by five-thirty, we weren't allowed to meet in the school holidays, etc, and that was very welcome at the start, although the family-friendly hours have to some extent really been much eroded over the years. It was hard, very hard, to juggle the children with the fact that my husband was an MS [sic] as well. In a lot of jobs, you can have flexibility, maybe one person going home early to pick up the kids and what have you. Well, we didn't have that. We both had to be there for votes and everything, so I did find that really difficult. With my first, when he was born in 2002, statutory maternity leave was just four months, and I felt that was all I should take, really – four months, just like everybody else was entitled to. I found that really difficult. It was a big adjustment to motherhood for me. I'd barely got used to being a mother and established breast feeding when I had to go back to work. So, I did have a very difficult few months, after I went back to work, because I was still trying to breast feed. I was lugging this breast pump with me everywhere, trying to express and everything, and it was very difficult. I remember once sitting in the car park in Pontypool and ringing my husband and saying, "I can't do this anymore, I'm going to have to resign my seat. This is just too much for me!" Because you're not getting any sleep, and a lot of people don't make allowances for the fact that you are a new mother. I still had the same people demanding meetings at short notice, particularly some in the Labour Party. I just felt really pressurised by it. Some things have gone backwards in terms of the hours we sit in the Senedd, and I think Bethan [Sayed] made some very important points about the difficulty of how easy, or not easy as the case may be, of having a young family and holding down a job like this. We need to do more to make it easier for women to make those choices because we want women with young children to be in the Senedd. I have often found it a struggle and I've often felt incredibly guilty, thinking, "Well, I'm not doing a very good job as an Assembly Member, I'm not doing a very good job as a mother." And I know that lots of working women feel like that. We can't rest on our laurels in the Senedd. We've got to keep pushing – not just within parties to make sure women can get selected – but to make sure people don't face those really tough choices such as Bethan has faced."

* * *

Chapter Eight

DIFFERENT VOICES, EQUALITY AND DIVERSITY

Having achieved gender equality in the Assembly of 2003, and then having that parity slip backwards somewhat, all the interviewees had views on the wider aspects of diversity, not just in terms of gender, but also in different voices, life experiences and social and professional backgrounds, ethnic minorities, disability, and equalities based on sexual orientation. They said they have seen changes for the better in these areas over the last twenty years and particularly in recent times, happening alongside external influences like Black Lives Matter and #Me Too.

The words 'politicians didn't look like me' featured a number of times, not just in a gender context but also in the fact that many of the women we spoke to came from backgrounds that had no political advantage or experience at all. They got to the Senedd through their own passion and effort, rather than through local councils or trade unions, though many did come that way too. What they all agreed on was that, despite the strides forward in recent years, there is still a long way to go and a lot of work to do to encourage and support diversity in all its forms in the Senedd.

ANTOINETTE SANDBACH

'I'd obviously spent twelve years as a barrister in London, I was articulate, and I felt that Welsh farmers had a lot of very incomprehensible paperwork they had to fill out and there was a lot of red tape that wasn't designed for people that had maybe left school early or had a long-standing connection to the land and had maybe worked it from a very long age. The average age of a farmer is about sixty, so things were very different when they started farming and there wouldn't have been the same levels of forms or bureaucracy that they're facing at the moment. And I felt I wanted to be a voice really. I think that's in the end what motivated me to stand for both the Assembly and Parliament – my legal training, and the fact that I did legal aid work, I mean I was dealing with people very often at the worst time in their lives. It's very interesting work because it's a wide variety, I think that's why very often you find so many lawyers going into politics, because they're used to handling cases and caseload, they're used to dealing with a wide variety of people from a wide variety of backgrounds, they're used to advocating on behalf of their clients. And so, I think there's a skill set that's very useful if you do go into politics, if you have a legal background.'

LISA FRANCIS

'We did seem to have an awful lot of lawyers, farmers, social workers, and people who'd been academics, and I was a bit of a rarity, coming from a small business background. I think it's hugely important that we have that diversity. Politics wasn't in my blood in the sense that it was something I'd almost stumbled into in later life. And that's part of the problem. There's a perception that people from certain backgrounds can't do it, or there was at that time. But diversity is hugely important and obviously having more female members, but it goes beyond that. It's about having more ethnic minority members as well, and people from different backgrounds, that's part of it. From a female point of view, we make up over 50 per cent of the population. It's hugely unfair that we're not properly represented in our legislature, so that needs to change. I was very fortunate that I had a real grass-roots knowledge of tourism from the work I'd been doing, which is so essentially important to the area I was representing, Mid and West Wales, and I'd previously been a non-renumerated Director for the Mid-Wales Tourism company. So, I felt I had a handle on stuff that was really important and which actually, at the time, the Welsh Government weren't really looking at seriously in my view. We'd had the Parliamentary Election of 2001, which was during the Foot and Mouth year, and that had highlighted the importance of tourism. But it was still very much at the back of the queue in terms of its importance to the Welsh Labour Government.'

JOYCE WATSON

'I had a sort of background of being hard working and honest. People would come to me more than I'd go to them and ask me to do things. But I wanted to do a bit more with my life, so I went into the clothes trade, and it was so slow moving compared to what I was used to [running pubs and a rugby club], I started reading. I got really bored and I decided that I would read biographies or autobiographies and became inspired then by what people had managed and convinced myself I could do it as well. So, the first thing I did was take my driving test and I passed it first time. And I thought, if I can do that, I can do more, so that's what drove me back into education. I didn't understand it at the time – coming back to the influence, there wasn't any, only what I'd picked up – I remember my father saying, when I was trying to get selected before getting elected, "You're doing really well," he said, "because the one thing that your mother and I can't do is, we can't help you with this. We don't have any influence." And I didn't understand what he meant. Because I didn't have any influence, and I didn't belong to any club or organisation, or anything, that's what he meant. There was no family connection to anybody, there was nothing, just my determination really.'

DAWN BOWDEN

'What it showed me was that, in Wales, we had a government that we could influence and that could change people's lives for the better in Wales. And for the first time I started to see directly what a difference that could make. And, while my colleagues in England were struggling to even get conversations with Government Ministers, all I had to do was pick up the phone and I could speak to the Health Minister. And we were able to change people's lives. And I thought, with my background and my experience, I could now see very clearly how that could work in the Assembly and how that could help to influence things in the Assembly. And I was also quite conscious, I think, of looking around the Assembly Chamber and thinking there weren't that many people in the Assembly, elected members I'm talking about now in the Assembly, that looked like me, that came from the kind of background that I had, that were trade unionists, that had come from very ordinary working class backgrounds, that hadn't been to university, that hadn't been a political "spad"[1] and hadn't worked for an MP or an AM before or anything like that.

---

1 Special Advisor, also written SpAd.

Somebody that just had real life experiences in coming through. And I thought we need those kinds of voices in the Assembly.'

VIKKI HOWELLS

'Gender equality is really important for me, but it sits alongside lots of other forms of equality. That's the way that I see it. I dip into it in different ways, such as we have a mentoring day where young ladies come down to the Senedd and they can be attached to AMs for the day. I've helped out with some of that and sat on panels to discuss with them how they could get into politics if they'd like to. But I see it as part of my role for championing equalities all round really. I work quite closely with a local group that's set up to support LGBT+ people, and for me, any work that I do around gender sits very firmly within that same sort of strata. I have lots of friends who are gay, and I've seen a big change in society over the last twenty years, particularly working as a secondary school teacher. When I was in school, I didn't know anybody in my school that was gay. Nobody felt that they could "come out" at that age, whereas over the sixteen years I was teaching, I saw such huge changes for the better. The biggest societal change that I saw during that time was the acceptance among teenagers of people who want to come out at quite a young age, people who may be transgender, as well. And to see that change and that acceptance is a wonderful thing. Anything that I can continue to do to champion that and get it firmly embedding in society, then brilliant. And another issue I'm concerned about is the lack of representation from the BAME community [in the Senedd]. And if we are putting All-Women Shortlists into seats in a "blanket-way" then, yes, we've got that vehicle for BAME women, but we haven't got that vehicle for BAME men, and some of them have told me they feel "doubly discriminated" against then because of their gender.'

LAURA ANNE JONES

'The first time round, Lisa [Francis] and I were split up from the [Conservative] Group a little bit, put down on the second floor while all the men were on the third floor. I don't know what to read into that. I think Lisa and I both felt that we started paving the way for other women to come into it. It was still a bit of a man's world at that point, but the Senedd itself at that point was 50:50 women/men, so things were starting to change, as a rule, across all parties, and the Conservative Party were starting to think we needed to do the same, so that was good. But we'd got there on merit, and I felt quite good about that, that we weren't put there because we were women. We definitely need more women, we need to be representatives of all backgrounds, all colours, creeds, whatever it might be, it's not just gender. It's very important that we reflect the country that we represent, and I do think we fall short of that by some way. It's great to see Natasha [Asghar] there and Altaf [Hussain] and Vaughan Gething, people paving the way, but we've still got an awful long way to go. It's massively important because it shows that other people can do it. She [Natasha Asghar] will be an important role model now to many girls, so she's got a lot of weight on her shoulders in that way. But we're all there to support her, and Janet [Finch-Saunders] and myself are really good at supporting each other, as the women in the group as well, and we're there if she needs us. It's important that we all stick together in that way. So, it's important she's there, as it is for Vaughan Gething being Minister, setting those pathways alight. All of that plays such an important role and I do think we need to reflect the people we represent.'

MICHELLE BROWN

'I don't think it is just in the Chamber, it is outside the Chamber. One of the things that struck me when I went into the Assembly was that Cardiff and the surrounding areas has quite a high percentage of Muslim people, so it's therefore got quite a high percentage of Muslim women, and devout Muslim women who wear a hijab. In the five years that I've been in the Assembly, I have only seen one woman wearing a hijab in the Assembly. Why is that? This is a place that supposedly is so pro-diversity, and goes on and on and on, there are reams and reams and reams of speeches, statements, policies, coming from both the Assembly Commission and from inside the Chamber, and yet I met one woman in a hijab. I can't remember seeing a black woman among the staff. There is one black man that I know of who is employed outside of the Chamber. The words don't meet the actions. They are encouraging everyone outside the Assembly to employ more people from ethnic minorities but what is the Commission doing? I wouldn't call that diverse, at all.'

LESLEY GRIFFITHS

'It is a big problem because perhaps people look to the Senedd and think, "I'm not represented there." The gender equality we did crack completely at one point and if you look at the population, it's not a population of men, is it? So, it's absolutely right that we have that gender balance. But it is a problem and what do we do about it? Certainly, I can speak for my own party. They've tried to influence and support people from the BAME community. It goes back to the constituencies. If you have a list of people to choose from, you might not get the gender equality or the diversity you would like to see. It's very difficult when you've got one member-one vote, but that's absolutely right, there should be one member-one vote. I go back to people putting their names forward and not feeling that they can't do it, and that's why I always say to people, "If I can do it you, you can do it." But it's about that confidence and that belief in yourself. I've got an area of Wrexham which has two of the most deprived wards in Wales in it – and I don't say that with any pride – but what I do say with pride is that the people who live on that estate and "do" for others is just incredible, and that is led by women. There is this amazing group of women, and we have a lot of Polish people in Wrexham, and we always have had. We had a Polish hospital on the outskirts of Wrexham when I was a child. I was at a virtual award ceremony last night in my constituency where the winner of the Independent Volunteer award was Polish and working with the Polish support centre in Wrexham. So, we have that diversity. I'd met her before and said, "You should put yourself forward for the Council," and she said, "Oh no, I haven't got the skills." So, I think it's about working with people to make them understand that they absolutely have got the skills.'

SUZY DAVIES

'This was the first time, if I remember correctly, that someone from the Conservative Party had participated in that group [a cross-party women's group] and was willing to discuss these matters with groups outside the Assembly, people like Women's Equality Network, working with Chwarae Teg, EAST for BAME women. It's important, because it's easy to say, if we don't take part, that the party isn't worried about equality. If you look, even with Boris [Johnson] and some of the comments of the past, we haven't created the right picture of the sort of party we are. That's what I would like to do during the rest of this term in the Assembly, see that we are serious about equality within the Conservative Party. The thing with Islamophobia, and I'm sure the same is true of anti-Semitism, some people are Islamophobic, definitely, and it's important to find them in our party in Wales, or wherever, and get rid of them, no second chances, out you go. There is no room for such hatred in our party and I don't want to be a part of a party that lets that happen. But there is another type of Islamophobia, too, people who don't realise what they are doing – ignorance, I'm talking about – but who are willing to listen and understand. We have to just get someone to speak to these people and explain, and if they don't get the message, well "bye-bye" to them too. As a Conservative Group – that is on behalf of the Welsh Conservatives – we've accepted the definition of the Westminster Group that Baroness Varsi has accepted, temporarily, hopefully, because that definition could be improved. I'm looking at it from a legal viewpoint and it's not perfect, it doesn't quite work, but there's a way to make it work. From the point of view of Wales, my message is that we are positive towards our Muslim communities, a lot better than in England at the moment.'

HANNAH BLYTHYN

'Your national parliament should be representative of the country and if you don't have people from different backgrounds, from all backgrounds, a diversity of representation, then I think it's weaker for it. There are things that parties can do in terms of perhaps positive action but there are also things that we can do as representatives too. There are challenges in terms of perhaps within party structures, in terms of how people are able to come through, and also in terms of perception that politics is for everybody, it is for people from different backgrounds and diverse communities. When I first was elected in 2016, and I became one of the three first "out" members in the Senedd, for a moment I did think, "Do I want to be pigeon-holed in that way?" Then I actually pulled myself together and just thought that actually it's really important because visibility in public life is very important, and you can't under-estimate it. Because if we're talking about perception, and people thinking it's for them, well you can't be what you can't see. I'm the only "out" woman member of the Senedd and

I certainly don't want to be the last. There's a responsibility on all of us, not just in parties, but as individuals to encourage more people to come forward and make it a place where they are going to want to serve. I was "out" to my friends and family and had been for years before I'd stood for election, but it is a big decision to do that in a public way. But it was a decision that I made. One of the reasons, when I was seeking election too, was that politics needs to be different and representative. I wanted a different type of politics and an honesty in politics, and it's about being honest about who I am. There were times when I was quite nervous about that, but when it hit home that I'd made the right decision was when, not long after I was elected, I went back to my old school for a visit and one of the teachers I didn't know came up to me and said, "I just want you to know that you are a role model for these children," and he referenced two of the students who were gay and they'd read about me on social media and it had made a huge difference to them. So, moments like that bring it home as to why it is important but it's not without its challenges sometimes.'

* * *

Chapter Nine

LEGISLATION AND CAMPAIGNS

From the beginning in 1999, the powers of the National Assembly, and then the Senedd, have increased and strengthened. The body has been able to do more and more to change things for the benefit of the people of Wales. The institution has been at the forefront in a number of arenas, and its individual members have fought hard, and sometimes alone, to change laws and introduce progressive legislation and thinking in all areas.

CATHERINE THOMAS

'Something that I feel was a major policy legislation was the free prescription scheme, which has really made a difference to so many lives. I'm aware of friends in England who have to make rather stark choices about the medication they can afford to buy, because they can't afford to buy everything that they should be having. I'm on medication for sarcoidosis and when I think, "Gosh, if I was buying this, how much it would add up every month?"... we are talking about a significant amount of money. So, for me, that legislation has actually saved lives, it's hugely important. Also, another one is the organ donation legislation, which again is making a difference, and again is ground-breaking. So, when I think of Wales as a small nation and what it is achieving, it's pretty significant and it is life changing, and I'm very, very proud of that.'

Health and creating equal opportunities have been an important element of the work of the institution's members. A number of members have followed their interests and their varying and important campaigns over the years:

KAREN SINCLAIR

Karen said that her greatest long-term achievement in the Assembly was the implementation of Type Talk machines for every political group office so as not to exclude people with hearing difficulties from reaching their representatives and from political life in Wales:

"So that's what we did. BT gave me a machine for each of the political parties and we trained up members within each of the group offices to be deaf-aware, and also, we trained up the people on our Assembly switchboard. In fact, we actually did a couple of deaf-awareness courses for them, quite apart from using the machine, for fronting the desks in the Assembly when they actually met people who were deaf. And then we formed a cross-party group on deaf issues, and we invited the various charities who worked on deaf issues, the Third Sector, to come and work with us. We were certainly the first part of Britain that introduced digital hearing aids and we were before England in introducing those on the NHS, and I'm proud of that. It really is something that I felt very strongly about, because an awful lot of deaf people couldn't really get involved with political issues because they weren't picking up. And it was not just politics, it was access to equal health care, access to local authorities, as of right rather than something they had to really struggle for. I was asked by my fellow ministers if I would chair a group that would identify what the need was in Wales in relation to severely deaf people, which I did, and that probably took a good six to eight months to do the research and come back with a report about what we needed to do. Because at that time, they only had about six fully qualified BSL interpreters in Wales, which was very poor, and our ambition was to bring it up to the European average. And I think we ended up with about forty-seven fully qualified interpreters, and I feel very proud about that.'

Other members have been able to garner cross-party support for their causes:

GWENDA THOMAS

'I led on the Social Services and Welfare Wales Act in 2014. It's a major Act and the process was long, but it gave a boost to my heart that we were able to establish a consensus at that time, because we would never have had an Act of that size through the Assembly, without building consensus, and without listening to everyone. And not just within the Assembly but outside too – such as bringing local authorities, the voluntary sector, health, everyone together to develop what would lead to the Act. I can't say enough about that and how important I saw it. I enjoyed that time a lot. And afterwards, seeing the Act have the Royal Assent, as they say, and becoming an Act for Wales. It was a splendid thing, to tell the truth.'

As well as social and welfare legislation, looking at cultural elements has been an important factor of the Assembly's external work:

NERYS EVANS

'I represented the Assembly as a body on the European Regional Council, and during my period of representing the Assembly (with Christine Chapman and the Labour Party), Westminster and the Welsh Government worked together to ensure that the Regional Council recognised the Welsh language for the first time. In November 2008, I was very fortunate to be the first person to speak Welsh in the European Regional Council. It was a wonderful thing, to do that and discuss afterwards with people from regions across Europe the support that was needed for minority languages across Europe.'

Some topics have been so important, so world-wide that they have raised support from afar, even from across the Irish sea:

ANN JONES

'The one big legacy is the fact that I took backbench legislation all the way through and got the Welsh government to put the regulations in as well. It took nine years, but I wasn't giving up, and that was to pass mandatory fitting of sprinkler systems into all new home builds. And I had tremendous support from Ronnie King, from the sprinklers' organisations, and from America and from Europe as well. And I'm the first person outside America to have the Jim Shannon Advocacy Medal for my work in fire prevention. And I had that in June 2017, which was just a couple of weeks before the Grenfell [Tower] disaster, when 72 people lost their lives. which I feel to this day some of them could have been avoided. So that's the one big legacy that I think I leave.'

Other campaigns may only belong to the representative's back yard, but they are just as important to every individual who is part of the campaign and who benefits:

BETHAN SAYED

'One campaign I'm really proud of is the campaign for Visteon pensions. Ford, the car company, created a new company called Visteon and the whole workforce was moved across to Visteon, and Visteon went bust, and finished, and all those people lost their pensions. Some faced a loss of up to 50 per cent of their pensions, and we fought and fought for years to ensure that Ford paid a deserving pension to them. We almost brought a court case against Ford because they [the workers] weren't going to get their pensions. But at the last minute, an agreement was reached with the pensioners to give them the largest part of their money. It took years of campaigning with people in Swansea, and going to England and Westminster, and lobbying around Bridgend, where the Ford building was. It's a campaign I'm proud of. I see myself as someone who can help these causes, to give power to people who are part of these groups to campaign on their behalf themselves. That's what I like most about being a member. A lot of people come to me [and say], "What? I can't do that. Oh, there's no way – you'll have to do it for me!" And I think, "Right, by the end of this, you are going to be more powerful, you are going to be running the committees and these groups." And that has happened.'

Within reason, issues relating to women are high on the 'things to do' list of the women who were Assembly Members, or are now Senedd Members, whether they are campaigning against injustice or campaigning for a better life for women:

JOYCE WATSON

'I came in hoping to make changes, probably naively believing I could make more changes than I could. But I'm pleased that I've managed. The legacy for me has been getting the plight of women up on that agenda. I make no apologies for the fact that I keep on campaigning to end violence against women and children, especially when I read a report yesterday that tells me that 50 women between March [2020] and now [November 2020] have lost their lives, and while that happens, I will keep on campaigning. And I make no apologies neither for bringing forward the plight of people who are trafficked or victims of slavery into this country that we like to think of ourselves as all-welcoming, which we are, but that we do nothing about. So, it's the disenfranchised, the silent voices. If I could help in any way to make the small change that makes a massive difference – that's what we do, hopefully, make a small change that makes a massive difference to those people – I will keep doing it.'

SUE ESSEX

'We did so many innovative things, the Children's Commissioner, the Older People's Commission, the Coastal Path. We were the first Fair Trade country in the world. We were the first country in the UK to reopen many of our railway lines – never been done since Beeching. Transport was a dream job for me, and one of the things I guess I was really proud of as well was the concessionary fares scheme, my baby from being in Cardiff Council when we did it for over-75s. And the important thing about that policy was how critical that was for older women at that time. I had so many letters from older women, not just older women of course, but mainly older women, who said it had transformed their lives. These were a generation who often didn't drive or couldn't drive because of illness, and they just had their pass – [it] didn't matter if they didn't have any money whatsoever, they had their pass and they could get on that bus and they could go to places. The letters were incredibly moving at times. They'd got on the bus in rural Wales, the buses then started again because they got some guaranteed money so bus routes were coming back, but particularly for women in rural Wales who couldn't drive or were worried about driving. So hopefully we were introducing policies that could improve the quality of life of ordinary people, everybody everywhere could access [transport thanks to these policies]. So those kinds of policies that are universal, I think, that can make an enormous amount of difference. That was one of the policies that I was so glad to see brought in.'

The work of the women of the Assembly on behalf of the children of Wales has been huge, tireless, and sometimes very difficult:

CHRIS CHAPMAN

'The big one for me was the "smacking issue" [the physical chastisement of children]. I mean that was horrendous really. But now nevertheless, that legislation is finally coming in. Julie Morgan and myself had a really difficult time in my final term in the Assembly. It actually made a difference, and the legislation is coming in. For that issue particularly, the thought that, as a Chair of a Committee – and I actually voted against the Government, that was unheard of – but, yes, it was difficult really. I didn't lose the Whip for the simple reason that if I had, we [the Labour Party] would have been in a minority. I was prepared to lose the Chairmanship of the Committee. I felt that strongly because it was something which we felt we'd been promised, that this was going to happen. It was an awful time really because it wasn't just some people in the Government who didn't like it, but it was actually colleagues as well because they felt that we were being disloyal. So, it wasn't a very nice atmosphere. But I don't regret it at all, in fact I'm very proud, because I felt that if we hadn't made a stand, that legislation wouldn't have happened.'

JULIE MORGAN

'One of the things I'm most proud about is getting through earlier this year [2020, is] the bill to ban the physical punishment of children, which I've campaigned for since 1997, when I became an MP. Children have less protection than adults in terms of physical punishment. You're not allowed to hit another adult but with the defence of reasonable punishment being there, an adult, a parent or a carer, can hit a child and have an excuse. I always felt this was very wrong. So, all the time I was in Westminster I was campaigning for that, trying to get Westminster to change the law, and we had several huge debates. It was an international movement, and I was very involved in that. A lot of the Scandinavian countries have got rid of this defence and so I visited Scandinavia a few times to find out what they were doing, but couldn't get anywhere in Westminster, and the amendment we moved was voted down. So, when I came to the Assembly, with new powers, I thought, "I can carry on with this." So, I just carried on with this relentlessly, saying, "We've got the power, we must do it." And then we did it and I took the legislation through earlier this year.'

As well as protecting, the members are proud of their record of listening to children, to children's ideas especially, and then acting on them:

HELEN MARY JONES

'I chaired the Children and Young People's Committee – which was a bit of a dream job for me – and was able to scrutinise government across a wide range of things. We went out and asked the children of Wales what they wanted us to ask the government about. It's quite routine now to do those kinds of consultations but we were the first to do it. I even got my committee clerk dressed up in a dragon costume to attract younger children to take part in the consultation and we did some really good work that led to "the right to play" being enshrined in law. Then there's a whole story to be told about the Rights of Children and Young Person's measure, where under Rhodri's leadership we had a really clear commitment to a clear piece of legislation. There was an attempt to bring forward a very watered-down piece of legislation that just would not have worked, and we were able through a combination of [sic – consultation with] of Swansea University actually. Their legal department brought together a group of Third Sector and legal experts who advised the backbenchers and we drove the legislation back to where it ought to be. That was really good cross-party working.'

SUE ESSEX

'We were much closer to the people than, say, you would be in Westminster, and that kind of dialogue that you could have, that reaching out to civil community was very important, so you got the best of the ideas and, if someone has a good idea, we can take them through. I was lucky in Cardiff. I could have schools in [to the Assembly] all the time, having a Cardiff constituency. There was a little girl from Cefn Onn School in Llanishen who, when we were talking about if you could do one thing what would you do, and she said, "I would plant a tree for every new baby." And I remember saying, "That's a wonderful idea. I'm going to see if we can do that." And we did! That ease with which a child from a school visiting feels that they can come up with an idea, and it was such a fantastic idea. I don't think that would ever work in traditional parliamentary situations, I really don't. It is easier to do that [with devolution], though it's not perfect of course, and we need it to change with devolution increased over the years. But I do think it was symbolic and also actual in terms of what it achieved in changing attitudes and changing polices and real lives.'

The Welsh Government still plants trees for each child that is born or raised in Wales – one tree in Wales and one other in Uganda. And in 2007, one of the Assembly's most important Acts was developed:

JANE DAVIDSON

'The big challenge that I had in that context was actually to deliver on the duty to promote sustainable development in everything that we did. It was a duty that had been given to us in the First Government of Wales Act in 1998, and the duty charged the Government of the day with putting forward a scheme to demonstrate how they were factoring sustainable development into everything they did. I was absolutely delighted that we were in partnership with Plaid Cymru for this, because I've always believed that cross-party working, where you've got a common goal, will deliver better outcomes. And what we created was a document called "One Wales One Planet". And everything we wanted to do in environment, in planning, in climate change, in energy, in housing was all included in that document. It was a vision for what a sustainable Wales would look like. So, my primary job was to demonstrate how the central organising principle of government could be delivered. Of course that meant that all those elements about kindness and compassion, cross-party engagement, caring about future generations, wanting to enable a society that was poverty free, wanting to enable an environment that was not trashed by either extraction, or pesticides or chemicals in the waters, wanting to enable communities that were safe and trusted and had jobs, wanting to enable people to be appreciated in equal ways irrespective of their background, wanting to celebrate the arts, the heritage, the life, the languages and the culture of Wales and wanting to be globally responsible. You can't have a separate agenda around environment, sustainability and housing. Sustainability has to be at the core of everything we do. In 2010,

I was invited to speak about this commitment to the 10th annual conference of The Sustainable Development Commission that took place in Bristol. And at that conference we heard that the incoming UK [coalition Conservative/Liberal Democrat] Government, led by David Cameron, had just dispensed with the Sustainable Development Commission overnight. It was literally on the journey back from Bristol to Cardiff that I wrote the core elements of what is now the Well-being and Future Generations Act. People love this vision of Wales. Those aspirations are all there now in the Well-being and Future Generations Act and once again Wales is back on the world stage because this is the first time in the world any country has put the Brundtland definition for sustainable development into law – development that meets the needs of the present without compromising on future generations to meet their own needs. The Well-being and Future Generations Act demands that Wales is a beacon. I do feel that time has been lost but maybe the Well-being and Future Generations Act enabled Wales to build the collaborations that we now need, to be much quicker than anyone else in terms of delivery.'

* * *

Chapter Ten

DEVOLUTION

Wales had a chance to vote for devolution for the first time in 1979, but the campaign failed that time. After the Labour Party won an astounding victory in the Westminster General Election of 1997, there was an unexpected second chance to win the campaign for devolution.

HELEN MARY JONES

'As a student of history, looking at the history in the '70s since working men had got the vote in Wales in the 1870s, we had never elected a majority for a Conservative government, but three-quarters of the time we got them because that's what the people of England voted for. And that was what started me, when I got to university, to begin to think about party politics and I got involved then in the campaign for the referendum [1979 devolution referendum]. It never occurred to me as a naïve nineteen-year-old that there would be people who would vote against some measure of self-government. So, I actually joined Plaid in the year after the devolution referendum was lost. I think the truth is that none of us then thought they would see another opportunity, perhaps not in our lifetimes, for a level of self-government for Wales and of course it was amazing when the tide of history turned, and here we are.'

On the whole, the former Assembly Members and the Senedd Members today support devolution regardless of political colour, and when the second referendum came around in 1997, a number of them had long been used to campaigning:

SUZY DAVIES

'In '79, I went out to campaign for an Assembly. By '97, I still voted in favour of having one, and that's where I thought I could use my skills and knowledge in the best way. But if you're going to be a candidate, and you're sincere about it, you have to take every chance to stand, and I can see it as a step to becoming an Assembly Member – some people think, of course, that being an Assembly Member is a step towards being a Member of Parliament in Westminster. I don't see it like that at all. They are equal and there is purpose to both places. I haven't been tempted to go to Westminster since being an Assembly Member. The Assembly – that's where I want to be. And, of course, I've been here during the most exciting period, because it has changed – let's be honest – from a bit of a "talking shop" to being a Senedd. I'm sure more power will come in future and there will be more members too, because they are needed.'

By the beginning of the '90s, especially after losing another General Election in 1993, a number of Welsh Labour Party Members were dissatisfied with the political situation in Wales after long years of Tory government in Westminster:

JAYNE BRYANT

'I felt really frustrated that in the early '90s that we'd seen another Tory government. All of Wales was voting Labour and I felt quite disheartened by that. That really made me feel sympathetic towards devolution because I just felt that Wales was being taken for granted. So, I joined a political party when I was seventeen, and I just wanted to be active. I did some work experience for Paul Flynn. I wrote to every local MP and Paul was the only one to take a chance on me. And then I wrote to lots of Assembly Members, when devolution started in '99, and Rosemary Butler answered, and I was fortunate to have a job with her in the First Assembly. It was exciting, exhilarating, a brilliant time, just feeling so proud that we had devolution and that I could work in a Welsh Senedd, a Welsh Parliament.'

The coming of devolution and the National Assembly would give an opportunity to more of our politicians of all parties to contribute to a brand-new institution in Wales:

EDWINA HART

'I always knew I wanted to be an Assembly candidate. I think people tend to forget what a good cross-party campaign there was before the devolution referendum, and I was very active in that. In fact, I keep in contact with some of the people from other parties who were involved to this day. And we had a very active campaign through the Wales TUC which I was heavily involved in, organising a rock concert, I recall, in Swansea – the then Castle Gardens – and various things like that, and it was good fun. And I didn't have any profile in it. I was just a worker. Because I think some people enjoyed the high profile in order to be a candidate rather than actually doing some of the work. And I suppose I was active as well with my friends in ensuring that they came out to vote. And we were so delighted, of course, because when we were sitting in Swansea and saw the results coming elsewhere and it was absolutely awful, and then when they heard the final result, we were just so absolutely delighted. It was a wonderful campaign to be part of and some of those cross-party alliances that were made before, I think, actually helped with the establishment then of the Assembly.'

JENNY RANDERSON

'I'd campaigned in '97 in the referendum for the establishment of the Assembly. I'm passionately pro-devolution and to me being a member of the Assembly, even though in those days it had really much more limited powers than now, it was such an exciting thing to be able to do. A new institution. We also watched the equally exciting development of civic culture in Wales – a national civic culture. And when I think of how devolution has changed Wales, one of the major ways is a much higher awareness of national identity and the Assembly had an important role in that.'

ANTOINETTE SANDBACH

Antoinette was a member of the Conservative Party in the National Assembly and was one of the few members that went 'the other way', namely from the Assembly to Westminster. She has now left the Conservative Party and is trying for candidature with the Liberal Democrats for Westminster:

'I think I've become a bigger fan of devolution, although I have my criticisms of it. I think at the time, I was a bit sceptical but I'm actually now a much bigger fan of devolution and of decision-making being made closer to all communities. Having had the advantage of both being at Westminster and in the Assembly, I think I'm someone who would very much push for devolution in an English context at a more local level as well. I think it's worked very successfully. I think one of the criticisms I would have about devolution is that there's no second [chamber], there's no revising chamber, so all the scrutiny work is done by the Assembly, and I don't think there's enough time that's able to be given to that. So, my legal background would say that the legislation isn't perhaps as good as it could be, and there isn't that constitutional break of a second and revising chamber. And I still feel there's been one party that's been governing in Wales since devolution, and I wonder whether that has led to a kind of stasis and stagnation in a way. The Assembly isn't big enough, there isn't really a role of a second chamber, but I wonder if there was wider constitutional reform, affecting the House of Lords for example, whether there may be a role in the future for the House of Lords as a second chamber to the Assembly.'

JANE HUTT

Jane Hutt has been a Labour Party Member in the National Assembly and then in the Welsh Parliament from the very first. But would she have considered being a Member of Parliament in Westminster if there hadn't been an opportunity to be an Assembly Member?

'Not necessarily. I suppose there are other life events. In the 1980s, I got married and had two children and, in those days particularly, there was still a big question mark about whether you could be in Westminster and in Wales if you had a Welsh constituency. So, I had thought about standing in my own constituency in Cardiff West in 1987, and I remember thinking – I just had one child [at the time] – that I would not seek selection. But I think we always had a very early urge to get devolution. I mean, the urge went back to 1979. I was involved in every stage, so I thought, "It's going to happen," and then you need to get involved in a political party to make it happen.'

Although the Conservative Party in England was vehemently against the idea of devolution, a number of Welsh Conservatives supported it completely:

LISA FRANCIS

'At the time, if I'd been elected as an MP, that would have been great. I would have done it, I have no doubt. But it was only later that I discovered that the Assembly was much better in that I embraced devolution. As a party we'd been told, when the Assembly was first mooted, that we should encourage people not to vote for that, and I think that in the run up to those Assembly elections I was very influenced by people like Nick Bourne in the Assembly elections of 2003, and I could see that devolution could only be beneficial for Wales, for any country really, because it meant government was closer to the people, more flexibility, and that we should campaign for more powers to be granted to the Assembly. That went against the grain of what Westminster Tories wanted. They certainly didn't want that. So, there was already the beginnings of clear blue water, if you like, with the sorts of people who were in the Welsh Conservative Group in the Assembly who'd been elected in 1999, and they influenced me a great deal. But, you know, campaigning in an area like Meirionnydd, Nant Conwy and Mid Wales generally, you could see the sense of it. Why would you want your health services directed by Westminster? So, I was already a committed devolutionist by the time I was elected.'

There were two different opinions about devolution developing in the Labour Party also:

TAMSIN DUNWOODY

'When I first become active politically in Wales, and was fortunate enough to be elected, there was very much a divide in the attitude by the politicians themselves, particularly in the Senedd [sic] who viewed Westminster as being obsolete, not directly involved, not really anything to do with us, and the Senedd [sic] was the most important place. There was another whole body of thought that still viewed the Senedd, because it was in its early days, as a training ground for Westminster, and certainly in the Tory Party that was a very predominant thought – OK, time served there, go to Westminster next. I don't see that's the way it is. I see the roles as being completely different and I think Welsh policy should be shaped in Wales for Wales, but there are issues which, I think, should remain at the UK level as a broad-spectrum issue. They're different roles. The one bit that is the same is being a constituency representative and that I love doing anyway, so it wouldn't have mattered to me whether I did that for Westminster or for Cardiff. It would be different in terms of policy and what you could achieve.'

Two years after the faction for devolution won in the referendum, elections were held for the new National Assembly for Wales:

ELIN JONES

Elin Jones, AS for Ceredigion, has been the Llywydd since 2016, but when she won her seat in the first Assembly, she was a young woman of thirty-three. So, what sort of experience was it?

'It was an incredible feeling and looking back at it now, I still can't believe the majority in that first election was 10,000 in Ceredigion. Only two other politicians in Wales had more than a 10,000 majority, Rhodri Morgan was one of them and Peter Black in Blaenau Gwent – and me, Elin Jones, Ceredigion, this little new politician. The feeling of getting a 10,000 majority, it was some feeling of invincibility at the beginning. And of course, it was an incredible period for anyone who believed in self-government for Wales, and seeing the Assembly being created. I remember the feeling of the first meeting, when the Queen was here doing the official opening, and although I'm a republican myself, the fact that the Queen was here didn't make that much difference to me, except that I felt like we were in India at the time India gained its freedom from the British Empire. I felt, right, now Wales is gaining its freedom from the British Empire. It didn't quite turn out as I expected it to in that romantic moment, but there was a feeling in a way that Wales was being given back to the Welsh and that we could decide our own fate. So, there was a feeling of elation for months following that election, and then of course it slowly dawned how restricted the powers that had been transferred to the Welsh Assembly were at that point.'

ELEANOR BURNHAM

Eleanor Burnham was elected as a member on the North Wales list. What were her feelings about the new institution?

'I have to say there was an "elephant in the room" from the start. I realised at once, looking at the figures, that the constitution was bad and also the money was totally inadequate compared to, for instance, Scotland and Northern Ireland, because when I first came to the Assembly, I went later to Belfast and also Edinburgh. Of course, I could see what was being driven on there, talking about figures, how things were developing. But I think from the beginning, that that lack of money – compared to what we should have had given the terrible poverty that still exists – [was] totally inadequate, and that it wouldn't work. So, that was one thing I saw, and I mentioned this in the [Liberal Democrat] Group, and no-one agreed. I didn't agree with a lot in the Group as regards a lot of things. I saw things completely different to them, because of the wide and different experience I had had outside of narrow politics, especially the narrow politics of South Wales and, more especially, Cardiff.'

Despite the lack of powers and money, others saw the advantages and what Wales could achieve and do differently within the strength of the Assembly:

JULIE JAMES

'I'm very pro-devolution. I've always been very interested in grass roots politics and I'm very keen on the notion of subsidiarity, so I think that decisions should be made as close to the people as possible to get them. All the things that I'm interested in are now controlled by the Senedd here in Wales, so I've never had a particular hankering to be involved in immigration or welfare, I'm afraid. I've always been much more interested in education and housing and social services, and that kind of stuff. And, of course, all of those things are controlled by the Senedd in Wales, and if you're an MP you have very little input in Wales into those kinds of day-to-day things. So, it was a very positive decision for me to do that [stand for the Assembly election]. I didn't try to get selected as an MP. I genuinely was interested in representing the place that I'm from. I was actually born here, all my family live here, but also the fact that I'm very keen on devolution and very interested in the topics the Senedd covers for us really.'

There are a number of different degrees of devolution and the first kind granted to Wales was weak in the opinion of some and not to everyone's taste by any means:

LEANNE WOOD

'I had mixed feelings if I'm honest. On the one hand there had been such optimism when we'd campaigned for the referendum and narrowly won it. I remember the campaign had been very much around us being able to provide a shield against the worst excesses of Tory powers, being able to build up an economy that was based on different values to the ones that were making so many people live in poverty, and we really believed that we could create something that was different to Westminster. And so, when I'd watched it from the outside in the first term between 1999 and 2003, I remember, for example, being horrified when the Queen turned up, first of all, and just thinking, "This is not what it was all about, this is not what we were trying to build," and so there were mixed feelings. I was, on the one hand, incredibly proud that we at last had a national democratic institution to represent people, but then on the other hand, it looked too much like what we were used to. It didn't have the teeth and the powers that the Scottish Parliament had, and it didn't seem to have the level of determination to get those powers. I think that the initial devolution agreement that we had was almost like an afterthought. Labour [Westminster Government] knew they had to deliver a strong parliament for Scotland, and they knew that they couldn't give something to Scotland without giving something to Wales. So, they gave to us the bare minimum. And I remember speaking to people who I knew in the Labour Party at the time who were trying to get a stronger institution, and they were very frustrated with the forces within Labour, that are still prevalent today. I mean, there are still tensions today between MPs and Assembly Members in terms of where powers should lie in the devolution settlement. I remember being in Westminster and having discussions in 2014 after the Scottish Referendum, after additional powers had been offered to Scotland, and we on a cross-party basis were trying to discuss what powers we needed here in Wales. And the block – apart from the Tories, where you'd expect a block to come from – it came mainly from Labour MPs.'

EDWINA HART

'I would hope the balance of power lies here [in Cardiff Bay] but we have incomplete devolution settlements. I was always extremely frustrated during my time [in the Assembly] because there were a lot of things *we* could have done over the things *they* [Westminster] could have done. I took the fire service back to Wales; I wanted policing [too]. The objections of course came from London and from Labour MPs, and Labour MPs would influence Labour AMs here and it was like they were trying to hold on to control. Well it was nonsense having it working that way, and I think we missed a lot of opportunities – when the Labour government was in – to fight our corner better about having devolved powers, which I think would have made this [the Assembly] much better in terms of public perception, and we should have tackled the whole issue of Local Government and how that should probably have been restructured.'

PAULINE JARMAN

'Obviously, I think, as a devolutionist, I'm very pleased that government has been devolved. But has it gone far enough? And I think no, it hasn't. I'd like to see law and order being placed in the responsible hands of the Senedd. So those are campaigning things that I will lend my name to, to improve the responsibility of the Senedd. Overall, I think that it did deliver some very positive outcomes, and I think recent events have proven that we're a small nation of three-odd million people, we're a very viable unit to govern. And I think that certainly the events [Covid 19 pandemic and effects] and the traumas of the last couple of months have proven that the Senedd has more than delivered its responsibilities to the people of Wales.'

ELEANOR BURNHAM

'To be honest, these days, I think we should be independent. I was learning towards that at that time. Because, in my opinion, the thing that has worsened in Britain is that fact – everything is located in London. When Thatcher came to power, she made everything worse, because she could see that some places in the north of England were being managed by Labour. So, she took the power and centralised everything. Look at the centralisation that has happened since then. And I think now that [Wales] should have "Devo-max" or be completely independent. The difficulty for Wales, I think is this: we are completely dependent at the moment on England for money. We have to fight for every penny. And of course, it's worse now because of Brexit. We'll lose the powers we've had. I can see Boris [Johnson] now taking the powers that were in Europe back to Westminster, and then we'll lose the additional powers in the Senedd. And, ultimately, I think one of the failings is the fact that everything is centralised in London. I don't see, for example, why we should waste our natural resources, like water, when we can't get our own water, and make our own money out of the water, and also be completely sustainable with wind and so on, and things like the lagoons in Swansea. No one is going to give us these things, are they, if we don't fight to get our own powers to control everything. We're going to be weak, I think, if we don't do something completely radical.'

HELEN MARY JONES

'The story of devolution for me is partly about hope betrayed, that in those early years we did so much, small things, like we established the Children's Commissioner for Wales, which was actually not small if you were a child, and you need access to your rights. We transformed early years education. We began to break down privatisation creeping into the NHS. And this is not a party-political comment, because all of this was being led by Labour ministers but often supported by cross-party committees who wanted those things to happen. We did ground-breaking things on the environment – the plastic bag tax, it's symbolic but it made a big difference. We are still recycling better than any other UK nation and that work to make that happen began between '99 and 2003. I think what's happened is that we've lost that, and some of it, in fairness, has been the impact of austerity, because those early governments had not exactly money to burn, but they had money to spend. But in the last administration, where I wasn't here between 2011 and 2016, and then this administration they've lost ambition, they're managing a decline. This is a choice. The fact that a third of the children in Wales live in poverty is a choice. It doesn't have to be like this. One of the things I'm kind of hoping is now we are in such a difficult position with Brexit happening, and what will be a power grab, a power grab from the centre against devolved powers – we're beginning to see that already – [is] maybe some of us can get that oomph back and say, look, this might not be amazing, this may not be the institution which has got all the powers, but it's ours, and we need to use whatever power it does give us.'

* * *

Chapter Eleven

WELSH NATIONAL ASSEMBLY TO SENEDD CYMRU

The Senedd Building

The first term of the Welsh National Assembly was held in Tŷ Hywel, located behind the present Senedd. Today, the building contains Senedd and Welsh Government offices but at the beginning, a lecture room in the building, which had space for all the members, was used as the Assembly's discussion or debating chamber. It was quite obvious that Tŷ Hywel wasn't suitable for the new institution's long-term needs. After considering and rejecting a number of options available at the time, discussion began about constructing a brand-new building suitable for the Assembly.

JANICE GREGORY

'There was talk about a new Assembly building, and I do know it was unpopular, especially among the North Wales members, who didn't feel that multi-millions of pounds should be spent on a building in Cardiff Bay. It was surrounded by controversy, really, the fact that it was a building that was unpopular with certain sections, the money that was being spent on it, you know, it was started off by one minister and continued by another. But like everything, like all big building projects, once it was up, people took ownership of it. But, yes, it was a bit of a tricky time really, spending lots of money on what people saw as a vanity project rather than anything that was practical.'

ELIN JONES

'I was completely frustrated that Rhodri Morgan at the time was constantly wavering about commissioning a new building and looking to see if it was possible to create some extension in the car park or something similar to that. It has proven its worth as a decision and I think we also made sure that it was done in a way that was fairly financially prudent. So, a budget of around £60 million was agreed at the start, and we were determined to keep within that budget. I remember I was on a cross-party committee that kept an eye on the building and how the building plan was going, and spending, and so on. Dafydd El [Dafydd Elis-Thomas] was chair, Sue Essex, Mike German, and me, I think. The Tories had refused to sit on it because they opposed the building and I think – this, of course, was following 9/11 – the spec' in terms of security and the building changed significantly and the budget had to increase somewhat. And I don't regret it at all, and I don't know anyone who regrets that expenditure, because it's not a Senedd for me, a Ceredigion member, to be sitting there for this period, but for a century and more [of] elected members of Wales to be sitting there, because that building is going to last for a very long time for us.'

The National Assembly held an international competition to choose the architect that would design the new building. The planning criteria required the consideration of its sustainability, including a design life of one hundred years, that the building used Welsh materials, renewable technologies, that waste and the use of energy be as minimal as possible, and that the building be an example in terms of sustainability. The competition was won by the Richard Rogers Partnership and the progressive new building for the National Assembly for Wales was opened in a national ceremony on 1 March 2006.

EDWINA HART

In January 2001 the plan was approved by Edwina Hart, the Assembly Finance Minister at the time:

'I love the building. I think that was the most important thing when we had all this nonsense. I always remember when we were talking about the building and what we were doing, we were all going around Wales and where it would be, I'll never forget that – what absolute nonsense. I'm a West Walian, right, but the reality was the Civil Service and government were here, so you had to have it in Cardiff, and if you're going to have it in Cardiff, where are you going to have it? Well, they did talk a lot about going up to Cathays – lovely building – but this was a modern building, this reflected a modern democracy, and I was always in favour of the building. And Lord Elis-Thomas and I battled hard to make sure that this building got up, because we had a cross-party group but of course some people didn't want to be necessarily involved in it. But we did and we saw the building to the end. I feel passionate about the building because I think the building reflects a modern Wales and it's so outward looking, but it also looks at our history as well. I love the way it's adjacent to the port building and there's something magical about its openness and everything.'

ELEANOR BURNHAM

'It was splendid! I think it was important to develop the credibility and importance of what devolution was. We went up to Edinburgh looking at that [Holyrood, the Scottish Parliament] – I didn't like that at all. It looked like Gaudi, and I don't think it was suitable. It looked like somebody had plonked something from Mars on it. But what we had was very good. The committee's institutions were odd – I felt like a mole in the new committee because they [the committee rooms] are underground, and I didn't feel like there was much air or fresh air or natural light. But I thought there was something perhaps – like the development of devolution in general – that was important. And we also had these additional places to do things like interviews, different people and different occasions, people socialising and meeting and so on.'

According to the Richard Rogers Partnership, "The building would not be an isolated, closed one. Instead, it would be a transparent envelope, looking out onto Cardiff Bay and beyond, making the internal workings of the Assembly visible and encouraging public participation in the democratic process."

SUE ESSEX

'It was designed to give equality, and Dafydd Elis-Thomas was very good about this, extremely good. So, the chamber ... everyone could be seen, and the language was never aggressive. It certainly wasn't when I was [there]. There was respect for people, and when you see what happens in Westminster – it's horrifying. Because there would never be anything that was personal or something in those days, and as I say, aggressive and unfair, other than in the bounds of normal politics. And I think women played an important part in that, because in a way you're just wasting [time]. Women's time is precious, isn't it, when you've got families, and you don't want any of that. It's just wasting time when we had important things to discuss. So, I think, intrinsically, that Assembly, both in the old building but certainly in the new building, was designed on [sic] that basis and, looking round the chamber – and women are the norm, you know – you always see that when you see the pictures. I think that's carried through. Even if the numbers ebbed and flowed a bit within parties, the style of the Assembly has been good in reflecting the influence of women in there.'

JANICE GREGORY

'There is absolutely no comparison between the old building and the new building. The new building is a statement piece for the people of Wales, and I always used to say, especially to school children when I took them around, "This isn't my building, mind. I have the great privilege to come here and sit in this building as an Assembly Member, but this building is not for me. This building is yours, you know, it's the building for the people of Wales." We should be enormously proud of our country and our heritage, and this is a building that is a symbol of that. It's not that difficult to persuade children, it's a bit more tricky to persuade older people who have a very fixed opinion about it. I don't think anybody would want to go back now to Tŷ Hywel, no, no way. It's a lovely building, it's fabulous. I used to love taking people [around the building]. They'd sit in the public gallery, and I'd say, "You do know these seats were made in Bridgend? And all the desks were made by the same company from Welsh oak. And then the artwork in the middle is called *The Heart of Wales*. Alexander Beleschenko was the artist from Swansea – that's a good Welsh name for you." And you could relate all these things and people were fascinated by it. Then the timber outside and the "mushroom". Rosemary Butler has a lovely thought on it [the "mushroom"] that she used to tell her school children. She likened it to a tree in Africa, where the elders would all gather at the base of the tree and then the tree would go up and the branches would spread out and spread the wisdom. And I thought, 'Well what a lovely analogy,' and then they could understand, and the chamber was the base of the tree.'

EDWINA HART

Edwina Hart thought it was necessary to keep a distance between the National Assembly's home and the Welsh Office in Cathays, as regards the legislative and the executive:

'Yes, I think that was important for the Assembly, but I was also a firm believer that the Government shouldn't be in this building either. I actually used to work a lot out of Cathays, to be here when the Assembly was in session, but I didn't think there should be government offices here, because I think the break should be there. I had an office in Treforest when I was Economic Development Secretary. I think it's important. There's the legislator and the Cabinet and I think there has to be a split. You have to talk to people and do things, but I think that's your business work, isn't it. This is your political domain.'

By now, the steps of the Senedd have grown into a very popular gathering place for all occasions:

ELIN JONES

'I remember that we thought to ourselves that this Assembly, or Senedd, will never quite prove its worth until Cymdeithas yr Iaith, farmers, and others come and protest outside. There must be protest as part of public life in Wales. The Welsh must have the confidence to protest against *us* too, rather than just protesting against what is happening in Westminster. We need to protest against ourselves. There doesn't have to be *too* much protest, but the steps of the Senedd are now a place of protest, public meetings. I remember one of the biggest protests that has been there is the protest by people from Aberystwyth, from the Bronglais area and the Bronglais hospital – organising buses coming down from the Aberystwyth area, a protest on the future of Ysbyty Bronglais at the Senedd. And there are all kinds of other protests, but also important national events. We've held several evenings there, because something has hit the world, and we've wanted to show our collaboration – our solidarity – with wherever tragedy has happened. And some of the big national events, our sport, have been marked here – winning the Grand Slam on more than one occasion now, and for me personally, welcoming Geraint Thomas during the National Eisteddfod, which was also in the Bay, where seeing those thousands – most of them Welsh speakers – was a highlight. Geraint Thomas received that welcome and that happened outside our Senedd. It has won its ground, I think. It remains unfortunate that Cardiff, our capital, is at the farthest south end of our country. There's not much we can do about that now but try to encourage and make this building a national building, not a building that belongs to the area around here, but a national building.'

Change of Name

The new building was called Senedd from the start. But on 6 May 2020, the name of the National Assembly of Wales organisation was changed to Senedd Cymru or Welsh Parliament after passing a legal Act to change the name.

NERYS EVANS

'[I'm] so proud to see that the Assembly has developed and evolved into a Senedd. Although it's just a name change, it reflects legislative power, taxing power. Obviously, I want to see more devolved power, I want to see us on a path towards independence and more strength here in Wales. So, it's good that we're on that journey, one step at a time, and I'm very glad that I've had the opportunity for one term to play a very small role in the history of the Assembly, now Senedd, of Wales.'

ELUNED MORGAN

'I think it shows that the organisation has grown up. I think it shows that the power is with them now that wasn't there at the beginning. And so, I think that is important, and perhaps important to the population more than anything else so that they understand that that organisation is going to affect their lives. Assembly – it's not quite the same status as Senedd.'

LYNNE NEAGLE

'To be honest, I would have been perfectly happy to keep it as it was. I don't think that constituents like us focusing too much on ourselves. In the end we had all the debate about whether it should be Senedd or Welsh Parliament. Many of my constituents now call it Senedd, and I'm quite relaxed about that. But at the end of day what we are called isn't what's going to make a difference. It's what we deliver for people, and I think we always have to focus on that, especially when things are going to be really, really tough for people now. We're in the middle of this pandemic, economic devastation is likely to be unprecedented and we always have to focus on that, really, what's going on in people's lives.'

DELYTH JEWELL

'I felt frustrated, just before the Assembly became Senedd, because I wanted the Assembly to just get the name Senedd. I didn't want it to be the Senedd Cymru, I didn't want it to be the Welsh Parliament, I just wanted the Senedd. But I'm still very proud. I feel that the Senedd has been the Senedd for years. Names, labels, are important and I hope that this will be able to help the people of Wales to feel more pride in the Senedd. That's not easy – that's a much wider discussion – but I hope that people will now see us as equals to the Scottish Parliament.'

JOYCE WATSON

'I supported it, I voted for it. I would have preferred to be called Member of the Welsh Parliament myself, I'm not hiding that, but the choice was made – Senedd – just the same way as there are other variations in other countries. People are using it, I've noticed, they are using it, but they do understand the word "Parliament" better. But that doesn't mean we can't get them to understand the word Senedd equally as well. And we've got a job of work to do there, and I'm speaking now as a commissioner as well. But I think the fact that we are a Parliament does change people's minds, and maybe it will help when it comes to asking for more members. That's a possibility. I don't know, in reality, when they see you as a little bit more than a local authority – and I'm not diminishing local authorities, they do a hugely fantastic job and are absolutely needed. I used to be a local authority member myself. But you need to see a separation, and at the moment I'm not sure people are seeing that separation.'

The Future of the Senedd

A committee, chaired by Professor Laura McAllister (see p 224), was commissioned to look at the Electoral Reform of the Senedd. A report by that committee was published in 2020 which stated that there was 'clear and obvious evidence that the Senedd is too small' and recommended far-reaching reforms to the structure of the organisation, including increasing the number of members, having a new electoral system and introducing measures to improve diversity.

LISA FRANCIS

'Certainly, we need electoral reform, for sure. All the recommendations bar one, I think, of the McAllister Report, I would totally endorse. I'm not very keen on the idea of job sharing. I don't think that works particularly well. But everything else in that report needs to happen. We certainly need it down in statute that we have 50:50 [gender] representation [and] a bigger PR element of voting people in. I think the size of it as compared to Westminster – Westminster is far too big really – so just have 60 members increase to 80, maybe more. Just the size of that means that you get to know other members very quickly. That helps.'

ELIN JONES

'I am a very strong believer in the recommendations that the Laura McAllister Report has referred to, namely, to increase the number of members in this Assembly, to do so through a system of voting through STV[2] – proportional representation – and to consider within that, then, making women's:men's quotas in terms of applicants essential, through legislation, and that we then protect the baselines for the future. And it is not difficult to do that, to get a quota through legislation, when on the whole it is equal at the moment. Protecting for the future, even though you are pretty much achieving that at the moment. It's more difficult for a parliament that is looking to introduce an average quota when they are not even close to average.'

JULIE JAMES

'I think it's undoubtedly true that there are not enough MSs to cope with the workload. Just to do proper scrutiny of legislation going through – we've only got a three-stage system and it really should be four if you're going to make good laws. There just aren't enough

---

2   Single Transferrable Vote

people to go round to do that piece of work. The Government itself is ridiculously too small. My portfolio is housing, local government, planning, child poverty, armed forces, waste, town centres, regeneration. That portfolio would be covered by twenty or more ministers in the Westminster Government. Albeit we're only dealing with a small population, we're still dealing with a breadth of topic. I think the Civil Service in Wales is too small as well. You cannot have creativity from people who just want to get stuff off their desks because they're overwhelmed with work. To be creative you have to have the space to be able to think. I think we've bowed to public pressure on what the size of the Civil Service should be and it's not adequate in my view. That's a very personal opinion that's not necessarily shared across the Government. However, selling that to the public is another matter altogether. Most people have no idea what politicians do all day. I think they think that we open fetes and talk on the radio.'

According to McAllister's report there are a number of good and valid reasons to increase the number of members in the Senedd:

ELUNED MORGAN

'I think the pressure on Assembly Members at the moment is immense. In general people don't like politicians and they certainly don't want to pay for politicians. So, asking for more of them is really difficult. But if people want people to do the work in a thorough way, which can save money for the taxpayers, I think it is important that we expand the numbers in the Senedd. The Senedd has much more responsibility now, responsibility for taxes, responsibility for legislation, in a way that wasn't there at the beginning, so there needs to be a change.'

LAURA ANNE JONES

'No, I don't think that we should increase the numbers of MSs in the Senedd. We've already got enough politicians representing us. We've got the MPs, who play an important role in Wales as well. We don't need any more politicians. We just need to get on with the job and use all the tools at our disposal in the right way first before we start doing that. There is so much potential in the Senedd if we use the powers that it has to the best of its ability.'

LYNNE NEAGLE

'It is very difficult to do a decent job of scrutiny with the numbers that we've got. We are incredibly stretched and I'm just lucky that, because I've been on Health so long, that I can kind of manage it really. So, I do think there is a strong case for more members of the Senedd to make sure that we do scrutiny properly and hold government to account. I don't think the public will want that, though, really, so I'm quite torn in that respect. I think we need to be very careful – at a time that is going to become especially difficult after Christmas when we start to feel the economic impact of Covid-19, of saying to people, "We want you to pay for more politicians." I think that would be a very difficult conversation to have with the electorate. But, objectively speaking, there is a good case for more members of the Senedd to do the job properly.'

On 8 June 2022, the Senedd voted (majority of 40 to 14) to increase the number of members of the Senedd from 60 to 96.

* * *

Chapter Twelve

COMMITTEES, MINISTERS AND LEADERSHIP

Committees

Although discussions happen in the Senedd's debating chamber, most of the interesting and important work takes place in Committee. Working together on committees is also an opportunity for the members who are in the opposition parties to be influential.

ANGELA BURNS

'I think the important thing to say about committees is that if you are on a good committee and you've got a good Chair, then you have the ability to make changes, even if you are a member of the opposition. Because in theory what should happen is you should drop your party a little bit at the door and actually work on the issue in front of you. So, I sat on committees where we'd come up with really good reports, recommendations, we listened to outstanding analysis and evidence and its being framed from a committee perspective, not from Conservative or Labour or Plaid or Liberal or whoever. And those committees are always really powerful, and those reports are really powerful. If a government has any wisdom – and I have to say they haven't always had the wisdom – they should listen to those reports because they know their own team, as well as everyone else's team, has actually investigated something really well and have come to a set of conclusions that really are worth taking on board. So, you get a real sense of achievement on a committee, and you feel you can make an enormous difference.'

Because of the small number of Assembly/Senedd members, the majority of the members serve on more than one committee or move quickly from one committee to the next:

NERYS EVANS

'Committee work was interesting. I was on the Culture Committee to start off with and then formed, with three others, a Broadcasting Sub-committee, the first time for the Assembly to have a committee on an issue that hadn't been devolved. So, it broke new ground because Ofcom was doing a review on public broadcasting and many back benchers [in Plaid Cymru] believed strongly that the Welsh Assembly should have a strong voice and an input in that process. And afterwards, that set a precedent to forming another broadcasting sub-committee to look at the press in Wales, in particular the print press, and I chaired that for a couple of months. But I didn't see the work through completely because I was promoted to Education Spokesperson. Certainly, that was a very valuable process for looking at topics in more detail. I spent the rest of the term on the Europe and External Affairs Committee, and also on the Economy Committee. Gareth Jones chaired that for the party [Plaid Cymru] and I was fortunate enough to step in to chair it several times when he was away from the Assembly.'

JANET RYDER

'I was part of the cross-party group on autism, and I think for my last four years I chaired that, and I was very pleased to do that. And again, you know, hats off to both Edwina [Hart] and Jane Hutt.[3] They both came, and they both talked to those cross-party groups, and they talked to the parents and they listened to them. And that's what people want them to do. They want them to listen, and they were both very open to coming and talking and listening, so that was really good. I went into Education as the Shadow Spokesperson and when I resigned that Education portfolio, within a couple of days, Ieuan [Wyn Jones] had come and said, "We want you to chair the Legislation Committee." It coincided with the next referendum and the next Wales Bill, and it was renamed the Constitutional Affairs Committee, because the Assembly needed a committee that looked at that kind of thing. After Rhodri Morgan stepped down from being First Minister, he became a member of this committee, so that was interesting to have somebody like Rhodri Morgan on your committee. And he actually said – on the last day that we held that committee together – he said. "I really think everybody should serve on this committee especially all ministers, because you don't know the half of it being a Minister."'

---

3   Former Ministers for Health and Social Services, Jane Hutt and Edwina Hart were two members that Janet remembers as being very willing to engage across party.

Ministers

The Labour Party has been in power in Cardiff Bay since 1999, apart from periods in coalition with the Liberal Democrats and then Plaid Cymru. Because of that, many more women of the Labour Party than any other party have had experience of being minsters:

EDWINA HART

Edwina Hart was the first Finance Minister in the National Assembly:
'I think a woman's perspective was important in all of the jobs. In terms of Finance, you always had to look at how you dealt with issues around equality within your budgeting process. And it was very important in Social Justice because I dealt with a wide range of issues that impacted on women. And in Health you can also see the impact you have by doing the right policies. And so you always had that perspective all the way through about the ultimate fairness in what you wanted to do, and economic development was the greatest challenge to that because of the inequalities that exist within that.'

JANE HUTT

'I've been a Minister for twenty of the 21 years [of the Assembly]. I was appointed by Alun Michael as the Health and Social Services Secretary, then Rhodri Morgan reappointed me, then Carwyn Jones appointed me. And then I left Government for a year from November 2017 to 2018. The role of minister did change. For the first few weeks and months, up until July 1999, we didn't actually have executive powers. It was still resting with the Wales Office Ministers, so we had a few weeks to learn the ropes of being Ministers. Then we became Ministers of the Crown. But the real change came for us when the Government of Wales legislation came through in 2006, when we separated to a legislature and an executive and then we had more executive powers. Before that we were members of committees, and it was a different relationship. We then gradually gained more powers. 2011 – the referendum, which brought us primary law-making powers – gave us a lot more responsibility, a lot more power to make legislation. Over the years, I've done Health, Social Services, Education, Finance, I've been Leader of the House, I've got Equalities at the moment, Crime and Justice now, so those are kind of new policy arenas for the Assembly and devolution. But it's always been a question of actually having the authority, and the credibility as a minister, to work as a team based on your manifesto and programme, to be accountable, and to enable the people of Wales to feel that you are working for them. It's no different to my whole political philosophy of how to work with people and to be accountable to people for decisions that you make.'

JENNY RANDERSON

A Liberal Democrat, Jenny Randerson was the first woman outside of the Labour Party to hold a role as a minister in Welsh Government:
'My role was Minister for Culture, Sport and the Welsh Language. I remember going into Rhodri's [Morgan's] office and he offered me the job and I said, "I can't do the Welsh language. I'm a really bad Welsh learner. I wasn't even born in Wales." He said, "Where were you born?" I said, "Paddington." He said, "The end of the right railway line!" You know Rhodri's ready wit! So, he persuaded me that a Welsh learner as Minister for the Welsh language would be a very good thing, because it wouldn't be someone who took it for granted. And actually, I became passionately keen on developing the language and I was very well advised and supported by a lot of people including the Welsh Language Board. And we had exciting times because Wales had never had a Culture Minister or indeed a Sport Minister or a Welsh Language Minister. We even had to form a new division of the Civil Service to support me. All they'd

done before was administer grants – they hadn't developed policy. So, we produced pretty major reports on cultural development and on the language – Iaith Pawb – which at the time and for years afterwards people used to refer to. So, it was worth doing, and I think we did some exciting and interesting work.'

JOCELYN DAVIES

Jocelyn Davies was a member of a number of committees. In her own words, she said: 'I think I've been on them all. I've been a member of all the committees nobody else wanted to be on.' She was Chair of the influential Finance Committee for a while but, during the One Wales Coalition of 2007, she was made a minister for the first time:

'I was probably the most reluctant Minister ever appointed. I didn't want to do it. Ieuan [Wyn Jones] really had to persuade me. I think that one of the reasons he wanted me to do it was because he said, "Well you had negotiated this document [One Wales coalition government document] and you know it best and you'll be able to keep things together." And he wanted Plaid Cymru's ministers to represent a range of people and I suppose being a non-Welsh speaker from the Valleys was important to him. And, if you've got someone who can do it, why wouldn't you? That's how I ended up Deputy Minister rather than Minister because I was so reluctant to do it. I don't have the confidence that other people have, so I didn't step into that very easily, although I think I was a good Minister in the end, and didn't know a lot about housing, but I soon learnt. There were definitely things that I knew most women would agree with, that we could band together on, I think. When I became Minister, Sue Essex had left the Assembly then, and we needed somebody to do a review of affordable housing, and I immediately thought, "Sue Essex would be the perfect person because she's not going to pull any punches and she's not going to go out there grandstanding either." So, there is that kind of feeling around other women that you are working with that, building up that trust is a little bit quicker, because you know what their motives are going to be. With men – for me anyway – they have to kind of prove themselves to me first that they are going to be worthy of that trust, whereas I think perhaps with women I do tend to take that for granted.'

SUE ESSEX

After a period as Chair of the Environment Committee, Sue Essex was appointed Minister for the Environment, Planning and Transport, and then Finance Minister. Rhodri Morgan said of her, 'She made a huge contribution in the Assembly, especially in the fields of planning and finance.'

'I chaired the Environment Committee when Peter Law was the Minister. They were difficult days in the Assembly, difficult for the Labour group, but Peter and I worked very well together. When I became Minister, Richard Edwards [Chair of the Local Government and Environment Committee, then the Environment, Planning and Transport Committee] who was only there for one term but was amazing, capable, and we worked well, and that was when we were getting powers on the railways in Wales for the first time. I think, because we were brand new they were so productive those years, because you wanted to do everything, you know, and obviously when Rhodri was First Minister that's what he encouraged. Environment and Transport was an absolute dream job for me. It was my love and my life before I got into the Assembly and just to have those two portfolios was brilliant. Rhodri was great. He said, "You do what you want really, just let me know last thing." So, we did break new ground. We planned a sustainable development commitment which went round the world, and has morphed into Well Being and Future Generations, and it's still here in the UN. So, I think that was massive for me, and the idea that the environment mattered, and it mattered in people's lives, it mattered in our policies.'

ELIN JONES

In 2007, Elin Jones was appointed Minister for Agriculture in the government of One Wales – the coalition between Labour and Plaid Cymru:

'It was an honour for me, as a farm girl from the west, to be a minister with responsibilities for agriculture and the countryside. It suited my background perfectly and I was eager from the very start to do something with the role, not just enjoy the job of being a minister. But I had a baptism of fire because I was appointed the week before the Royal Welsh. I was only able to go to the Royal Welsh on the Monday as I was flying to New Zealand for a three-week holiday that had been arranged a long time before. I spent a day at the Royal Welsh and made thirteen speeches, to all intents and purposes, in my first day in the role. And I had to take a decision that was a very controversial decision. Welsh Government policy was to destroy cattle because of TB. There was a bull called Shambo [that had been adopted by the local Hindu community of Llanpumsaint as a sacred animal] that had TB and was going to be taken, but the owner in Skanda Vale refused to allow that, and the case had gone to the Appeal Court in London. I had the phone call at the Royal Welsh to say that the case had been won by the Government and that Shambo had to be destroyed as per the TB policy. And so that was the first decision I had to take as Minister, and it was a very controversial and very public one.'

Elin went straight from the Show to New Zealand on her holidays but two days after arriving she had a call to return because foot and mouth had broken out in Surrey:

'Immediately after coming back, I had to join the Cobra meetings, which were being chaired by Gordon Brown, to deal with the foot and mouth disease, in August 2007. I remember, on the Eisteddfod field, I needed quiet to take part in a phone conversation meeting with fellow ministers in Scotland and England, and the only place I could find was in the Bardic Circle. It's possible that this is the only telephone meeting of agricultural ministers in the UK to take place in the Bardic Circle!'

More recently, the Environment, Energy and Rural Affairs portfolio, which includes agriculture, fisheries, animal health and welfare and food and drink is in the hands of the minister:

LESLEY GRIFFITHS

'The [past] five years of this portfolio [2016-2021], has been completely shadowed by Brexit. Every part of my portfolio is completely bathed in EU legislation, EU funding, so I've had a massive focus on Brexit and leaving the European Union and now the difficulties we're facing through leaving the EU, and the opportunities, which are very few, but you have to grasp those opportunities as well. When I came into the portfolio at the beginning of the term, I was a bit unsure. I came from a completely non-farming background, the [Wrexham] constituency has half a dozen farms in it, we haven't got a coast, so I knew very little about fisheries, which is incredibly complex. But I absolutely love it. I think, because I've had five years of it, I've just got involved in it all. I remember my very first farming conference. I think I'd been in post for about a month, and I went to speak at one of the farming unions' conferences in Aberystwyth University. I went on the platform to speak and the only women in the audience were myself, my private secretary, the chief veterinary officer and two others, and the rest were male, probably out of 90 people, maybe a hundred. I had not been used to that in previous portfolios, and somebody said, "Well you'd better get used to it!" But I have to say there are some amazing women in agriculture who really now put themselves forward. You know, quite often you go on a farm visit and they are the most hospitable people I've ever come across. The kitchen table will be laden with food – it doesn't matter what time you go – and you are expected to eat bara brith and Welsh cakes and scones and sandwiches, which invariably the woman has prepared while also milking, making sure the sheep are OK, getting the children off to school and then going to their teaching job. I mean, they are just incredible. One of my interests has been young farmers, as well, and it's great to go on a farm and see the young women who've been over to New Zealand to do some shearing, they've been to Harper Adams and got their degree, they're doing the Nuffield Scholarship, they're telling their dad, "No, Dad you need to be doing it this way now," and the dad really wanting to learn from them. It's fantastic.'

EDWINA HART

After a period as the National Assembly's first Finance Minister, and then as Minister for Social Justice and Regeneration, Edwina was appointed Minister for Health and Social Services:

'In terms of the Health portfolio, I think people found health very difficult as ministers. It was hard even though they enjoyed doing things, but the Health Service needed reform and it needed to be got a grip of. So, when I was appointed Health Minister, I thought, "Here we go." You've got to have good people around you and I was very fortunate to have a very good chief executive most of the time – Sir Paul Williams – and we knew what we wanted to do in terms of the Health agenda. But Health was the one that impacted most when you were an Assembly Member, because everyone thought across Wales that they could come and see you in your surgeries in Gower, because they had a health issue! So, these people would come, and I'd have to say, "I'm terribly sorry – I can't deal with this. You email me at my ministerial address, and we'll deal with it." And what I found in Health was ... I've always read all my correspondence as a minister. Now, as Finance Minister, there wasn't a lot; local government was a bit more; Social Justice had quite a lot; and when I came to Health, I used to read it all. Some health officials didn't want this done and preferred that it just be marked up and some put into a big pile for the correspondence unit to be answered by civil servants, and not seen by you, who'd receive just a few. Well of course I stopped all that, I saw them all. And once you saw them all, you'd start to see a pattern emerging of where the issues were. And of course, then I'd insist on seeing my replies, and they'd say, "Oh, there'd be far too many replies for you, Minister, there'd be far too much to get through." And I thought to myself, "If I'm up until two in the morning, I'll get through this and prove you wrong." So, I used to do all that and you did get a good idea. During this period, I formed an excellent relationship with the Royal College of Nursing and of course I started doing "on spec" inspections. They didn't know I was coming to a hospital, and you'd see these people scrambling down the stairs, men usually, putting their jackets on and rushing to the door because you'd appeared somewhere, and you'd like to have a look around. I always remember the Chief Nursing Officer and I did a trip out to Llanelli, and they were in an absolute panic, the Chief Nursing Office and me just appearing. And of course, where would I go? I'd send my driver in to check how clean the men's toilets were, and I'd go into the Ladies! Well of course this soon got around. So, all those types of things that members of the public had written saying, "This is wrong why is this going on?", you could actually deal with if you did that on the hoof.'

Leadership

Over twenty years have passed since the National Assembly met in Cardiff Bay for the first time. In 2003, after all the Twinning of the Labour Party and the Top of the Plaid Cymru List, there was an equal Assembly in terms of the sexes – the same number of female members as there were male members.

KIRSTY WILLIAMS

Kirsty was elected as leader of the Welsh Liberal Democrats in 2008:
'I guess it was a natural, dawning realisation that the party needed a change and how was that change going to happen. And I'd spent a little bit of time umming and aahing, didn't know what to do, didn't know whether to go for it. I think part of that was a lack of confidence in the sense of, "Who do you think you are? Why do you think you can do that better?" or "Why do you think you can do that at all?" There was growing pressure in the party for change and a lot of support, you know, "You can do this." In some ways I was very reluctant. My husband definitely didn't want me to do it. He'd been incredibly supportive, never complained about late nights, but was very unhappy about me doing it and felt it would be too much for the family. And then I went – I can't remember quite where it was – and I heard someone speak about the role of women in politics and the role of women in public life, and that person said – and it wasn't directed at me – one day some women are going to have to step up to the plate and do this, and why would you think that's ok to pass that responsibility onto another woman. That struck a chord with me, and I thought, "OK I'm going to do this."'

LEANNE WOOD

Leanne tried for leadership of her party in 2012 in order to make Plaid Cymru more attractive to people in the South Wales valleys:

'I didn't really want to lead the party. It wasn't something I'd set out to do. To be honest it wasn't even something I'd given much consideration to, until Ieuan Wyn Jones stood down and there was a vacancy. I took a bit of persuading by colleagues and friends to run. Again, I think it's just that assumption that, "Well, what have I got to contribute to this?" But I was convinced that there was a political project worth trying to build. So, I put myself forward on the basis that I wanted Plaid Cymru to become a party that was more accessible to a wider range of people, that I wanted Plaid Cymru to be a party that took more seriously the ecological challenges that we face and to think more deeply about the green agenda. And also, as a socialist, I wanted to work in a way that ensured that our socialist aims – that we're all committed to as a party – were reflected more strongly in our manifestos. Given that this was a clear political project, and the idea of making Plaid Cymru a party that was more attractive to people in places like the Valleys, places where we might not have had such strong representation before, made sense and so I stood on that basis. It was a big shock if I'm honest. I really wasn't expecting to win, and the general commentary was that I was an outsider. But some imaginations seemed to be captured as part of the campaign. I was able to offer a set of policies that fitted in with the roots of the party. I'd drawn back to look at what previous thinkers and contributors to Plaid Cymru had said in the past and tried to draw and make relevant their writings to the current situation, which was post-banking crash. So, what could we draw on from the past that could give us some solutions for the future? And I managed to convey to people that we actually had a lot to draw on. And even though things were looking pretty grim on a global, financial and economic basis, there were some pieces of hope that we could put together to offer something different and that was around offering what I termed at the time "real independence". I stole that [term] from Raymond Williams, but it was meant to convey something more than just constitutional independence. It's about a state of mind and if we can think independently, be independent in our own lives and in our own communities – Wales is a community of communities – all of that adds up to independence as a whole. So, it's just about being prepared to do more for ourselves, being prepared to stand on our own two feet and be independent in a very real way, which then would hopefully contribute towards being independent in a constitutional sense, as well. People seemed to like it.'

Although Labour has more women with ministerial experience than any other party in Parliament, as a party in the UK, they have never had a woman as leader:

EDWINA HART

'I deliberated a lot [about] whether I wanted to stand or not and I was persuaded by colleagues, probably against my better judgement because I wasn't sure I ever wanted to be First Minister as desperately as other people seem to want to be First Minister. But my colleagues said to me, and especially some colleagues in the trade union movement, "Well, we actually need a voice that resonates with the public." And so I decided, after a long hard thought, that I would go for it. I always knew in my heart of hearts that I'd never win, because when I look at what happened in my own selection, and I look at what people feel, I'm not what you expect at all – fat, middle aged woman, never got a degree, talks a bit like this – and well, of course, the others, their voices, the way they talked, the way they'd been, etc. Now that view was a view that was held by members in the party, I think, about what they felt a leader should look like. I think there's an element of that all the time. So, I went in, and I had a lot of support from the trade unions, but I always knew at the end of the day I wouldn't quite do it. But I'd never fallen out with Carwyn [Jones] or Huw [Lewis] during the campaign. However, there was a pretty vicious campaign [that] went on against me from certain elements from Carwyn's side, but I have to say that Carwyn, when I lost – and I lost very gracefully, made a nice speech without a pile of notes – was very good to me. We got on fine. He respected the fact that I was probably more loyal to him in that Cabinet than perhaps people that had supported him. People said, "You should move her out, get her out of Cabinet she'll be trouble," but he actually remained true to the principle with me that I'd lost, I'd fought it fairly, he and I had always got on before, and I carried on [in Cabinet]. There was a momentary sense of disappointment [at losing] and when I look back now, I wish in many ways that I had been First Minister, because I don't think that some of the things that have happened would have happened, as I'd have dealt with things differently.'

SUZY DAVIES

In 2018, an unexpected opportunity came for Suzy to stand for leadership of the Conservative Party:
'Andrew R. T. Davies resigned and the first thing I thought was that competition was needed within the party, because that is part of our having a Welsh leader instead of just being part of the bigger party. Also, I wanted to do it in the next Assembly, but Paul Davies came forward and we have a lot of common ground, in a way, coming from the same place in the party from the viewpoint of being moderate and for Wales. Also, I wanted to

appear as a Conservative woman in charge that didn't look like Margaret Thatcher, just to show women – and men too – that it was possible to be a leader who didn't look like you expected, didn't sound like you expected, and perhaps wasn't a leader in the traditional Conservative way. I'm a team player, and I listen, and I look for opportunities for people to come through and have their say, instead of looking at the five men in the corner who organise everything in our party at the moment. And also, to show it's not necessary to be like Churchill, shaking his fist and talking. I wanted to bring the party to a more contemporary place and point out that it's possible to make mistakes and apologise. It's not necessary to be perfect.'

ELUNED MORGAN

In the same year, Eluned tried for the main job – the leader of the Labour Party in Wales and First Minister of Wales:

'In a way, it was too early for me, because I'd only been in the Senedd for two years, and had only been a minister for one year, and the fact I hadn't had a lot of ministerial experience. But what I didn't want was to lose the opportunity. In a way, what motivates me is not the big job but not wanting to look back over my life and think, "What if...?" That's more motivating than anything. I also thought it was important to have a woman on the list. It's been difficult for women throughout history to have that experience of putting yourself forward, and it's still true within the Labour Party even today. If we don't put a system in place, women just aren't going to go through the system. It's still true today. But, having said that, I think it's really important that I understand I have weaknesses. Perhaps it was too early for me, perhaps I didn't have experience, and I think you have to make sure that you understand it's not something against being a woman, but perhaps that people don't like you personally, and you have to accept that as well. You have to be careful not to put a label – "It's because I'm a woman." Perhaps it's because they don't like my politics, or don't like who I am, or just that they think I've gone too soon. And looking at what Wales's First Minister [Mark Drakeford] has gone through this year, with Covid, I have to say I would have found it very tough. And I think the right leader was elected.'

* * *

Chapter Thirteen

CONSENSUS AND COALITION

When the Welsh National Assembly was established, the first intake of members had hopes and ideals as to how the new institution would operate. The female members in particular were enthusiastic about fostering rational and consensual discussion in the Chamber and in committees, rather than the bad-tempered adversarial politics that is part of the daily political system of Westminster.

JULIE JAMES

'Behind the scenes in the Senedd, with the exception of the minority parties that were elected in the last election, almost everything we do is consensual, even with the Conservatives. Because, actually, politics in Wales is quite a lot left of centre than where it is in England. And we are able to work quite consensually over almost everything. There are nuances we argue about – the thrust of the curriculum changes we have been doing, the elections and Local Government Bill that I have put through, the Rented Homes Act, and so on. They are 80–90 per cent consensual, and that's because we have a soft influence on the political discourse of the country.

I think it's hidden from people, and it needs emphasising because it would allow more people to understand why it's a privilege to do these jobs, because you really do get a chance to do that and trying to get young women to see that if they have something they care about vehemently, they can get that thing to be prominent.'

But not everyone agreed with the above opinion:

ANGELA BURNS

'For me the greatest shock to the system was how the Assembly side worked, because as somebody who wasn't overtly political and somebody who's fairly centre, I'm definitely centre-right. And somebody with my kind of background, I'd always assumed, and I just thought that, once the elections were over, once we'd done our striving for our political viewpoint, when you actually had a problem that you'd perhaps work more together, and that was probably the thing I had to "unlearn" very quickly. It was an idealistic view. The thing that really brought it home to me was when David Melding put forward an LCM [Legislative Consent Memorandum] and it was to do with young people, and it was something of real benefit with mental health and young people, and it was voted down because he was a Conservative. I remember at the end of that vote thinking, "Oh my God!" Because, from my point of view, what I saw was a really good idea which would have developed into a policy that had real potential and could have made an enormous difference to people's lives. I felt unbelievably cross, and I felt that the people of Wales were being short-changed. I thought it was incredibly short-sighted and in my political life going forward, I have tried where possible, when I've felt it's appropriate, I have given my support to other parties, and other policies. If somebody comes up with a really good policy, just because it's not my idea, if I think it's really good and could make a big difference, I will always fight [for it] within our party. I try very hard not to just say, "Well, that came from Labour..." or "That came from Plaid..." or "That came from an Independent. Let's just dismiss it out of hand." Because I think that doesn't help the people of Wales.'

DELYTH JEWELL

Delyth was a researcher for Elfyn Llwyd, Assembly Member and Plaid Cymru Group Leader in Westminster, before taking her seat in the Assembly:

'It's interesting. One of the things that has surprised me most with the work in the Senedd is [that] I expected it to be easier to work across party than it was in Westminster. I think people want to work across party but, because there are so few people, and because everybody's so busy all the time, and there's no physical place in the Senedd where people gather in the same way as in Westminster, it means that the opportunities somehow don't arise in the same way, and that's something I think needs changing. We should have more members and I think then there would be more space to do things outside the usual channels, that don't have to happen officially to begin with. That's how we succeeded in getting change in the law [in Westminster] but somehow those opportunities aren't there in the same way in the Senedd, and that's something other than I expected.'

JOYCE WATSON

According to Joyce Watson, the consensual nature and tone of the National Assembly has declined over recent years:

'It was [consensual]. Not now. This term has been horrendous, in terms of UKIP particularly, coming in and then changing to Brexit. It is not the pleasant place, or as pleasant a place as I walked into in 2007. There's no question about that. It was much more collegiate in 2007. Now, you need challenge in politics, of course you do, and

I'll challenge anybody myself, but you don't have to be nasty about it. You don't have to be personal – you should never be personal actually – about it. And we've lost that somehow. It's not easy, and I've had my own personal attack from UKIP[4], and it wasn't pleasant in any way. And it wasn't helped when I complained that it was a sexist attack, and personal, and broke all the rules. And it was not helped when the then Standards Commissioner said it was OK. That was never going to be OK by me. And I thought, "You're not going to say this." How can I ask young women, which I've done all my life, to come into politics, and let that be OK. It can't be OK.'[5]

JENNY RANDERSON

'Just over a year after the Assembly started, the Liberal Democrats went into coalition with the Labour party under the leadership of Rhodri Morgan. Of course, there were people in the Lib Dems who were worried about that coalition, and we had to have a conference to agree to it and so on, but it was very heavily endorsed by that conference. I was in favour of it. I mean you've got to ask yourself why you're in politics. Sometimes people are in politics because they care passionately about one thing and as long as they're able to pursue that agenda they're not looking necessarily to be in government. But my interest was always very much broader, it was more sort of a way of life, a way of treating people, that I was interested in, and so I was very certainly supportive of the idea of a coalition. I was also in the coalition [government with the Conservatives 2010-15] in Westminster much more recently, and

---

4   There was a cross-party women in Democracy group in the Assembly – a closed group – a place for the members to discuss the reality of being in the Assembly, the challenges and problems, the tensions in every party.

5   In 2018 Leader of UKIP in the Assembly Gareth Bennett AM, created and shared a demeaning video of Joyce Watson on YouTube. He was later excluded from the Senedd and had his wages docked for a week.

I would say it was an easier coalition in Wales. The aims of the two parties were more easily linked in together, coordinated, and also it was easier because we were next to each other. I used to rely a lot on Edwina Hart for finance, for cultural projects she wanted to start, and so on. She was in the next office. It's a lot easier to develop joint plans if you actually know each other.'

JANE HUTT

'I've had two periods of time in coalition with Liberal Democrats and Plaid Cymru as a Minister, and these have been also very interesting important times, and particularly with the coalition with Plaid Cymru, working with Jocelyn Davies as the other the Plaid Cymru Minister at the time, working with her to actually forge the One Wales Agreement. So those were pretty unique times to be a minister and pretty important. We felt that we were two women crafting this new accord between two political parties. But obviously I've been a minister through minority periods. I think the most important [aspect] of being a minister was when I was Finance Minister. We were a minority Government and I had to forge agreements with other political parties in order to get our budget through, and I did that six times, with Plaid Cymru, Liberal Democrats, also with both of them at one stage. And that's about creating bridges to make sure you're on the same side in terms of getting policies and funding decisions through."

The period between the 2007 Election and forming an agreement between the parties was a stormy one. The way forward wasn't obvious or easy and Plaid Cymru, as the second largest party, had to make decisions between supporting an One-Wales-Agreement – the 'rainbow' coalition of the Conservatives, the Liberal Democrats and Plaid Cymru – or supporting a One Wales coalition agreement with the Labour Party:

JOCELYN DAVIES

'It was interesting the day that the deal was struck because we had the document. Jane [Hutt] and I had negotiated the document and the only time that Rhodri Morgan and Ieuan Wyn Jones were involved in the negotiations were [on] things that we couldn't agree with. So, anything we could agree, I had a little reference group that I'd go back and talk to, so did she. Everything that we couldn't agree [on] might go to Rhodri and Ieuan to talk about. Anyway, the document was virtually completed. Rhodri and Ieuan were meeting together privately, so nobody else was there. So, Jane Hutt said to me, "We'll give them twenty minutes and then we'll go in," – this was into the First Minister's office now. Twenty minutes passed and she [Jane Hutt] just goes in, opens the door, and goes in, so I follow her. Rhodri Morgan was on this sofa, shoes off, and he's saying, "Oh hi Jane, hi Jocelyn." Ieuan's sitting over there, he really looks miserable – *oh this hasn't gone very well* –but Rhodri's perfectly comfortable: "I was just talking to Ieuan, and we were just talking about the options in front of us – New Zealand option – remember that? This idea of you'd have this New Zealand option where you'd [Plaid Cymru] just agree to vote for them on the confidence votes, or we could do this or..." So, I just said, "Rhodri, I've got a coalition [Rainbow coalition] waiting for me elsewhere. It's a coalition [with Labour] or it's nothing. I don't care who's asking or who's agreeing. It's that or it's nothing." And Jane Hutt said, "There we are. Coalition then." And they went, "Yeah, ok." It was like a scene out of a sit-com because both of those men wanted the other one to ask, they wanted the other one to say, "Shall we have a coalition?", so they were talking around it. They wanted to be able to say afterwards, "He asked me."'

EDWINA HART

'I was in coalition with the Liberals, which was all right in the beginning. I got on fine with Jenny Randerson. Peter Black was my Deputy Minister with responsibility for housing and he was first class, and I always knew what he was doing. He'd always do the business and he did the work. I found that quite easy. It wasn't an easy coalition from the point of view of all the problems with Mike German but that aside... And the coalition with Plaid [Cymru] I quite liked. We couldn't form a government, you see, and we went into coalition, and it was a good coalition from the point of view that we had such a detailed agenda with the coalition. Because I negotiated some of the Health stuff like a rural health plan and various things like that. And after that – we had differences obviously – but we all actually made it work, I think, for the greater good. But there were some in the party that didn't want it. And of course, we had to have a conference to say everything was all right and I didn't go – I was actually doing a surgery in my constituency. Well, the political world was changing. We had to guarantee the future of devolution and guarantee an agenda that we wanted, not an agenda that the Tories would have any part in. That's what you do, that's what you learn. You don't have everything from a trade union negotiation. You don't have everything you want. You get to the best deal you can and hope that that'll be enough. And that's quite important. I don't think sometimes there's much experience of that. Women are much better at working in that way, and I think that coalition worked from that point of view because Jocelyn [Davies] was taking quite a lot of a lead on the Plaid [Cymru] stuff on some of this, and it was just good to do it. And we had some fun in government with them, you know, and we were – all of them – quite open with each other. But once the election comes, of course, things change. I think, as there was a great understanding of what the health agenda was, we discussed what we needed to do in Cabinet, briefing Cabinet colleagues and that was an enormous help to me in getting any changes I wanted in Health. OK, there were lines that people didn't want to cross over but I felt there was a good adult discussion going on, and it was a good adult discussion.'

HELEN MARY JONES

'When we had the 2007 Election – a pretty good result for Plaid [Cymru] – the coalition discussions, and I ended up shadowing Edwina [Hart] in Health. She brought me into all the crucial meetings. We made decisions and then went and told Rhodri [Morgan] and Ieuan [Wyn Jones] what we were going to do, and the biggest of those [was] taking the market out of Health. We worked very closely together, we stopped private finance initiatives in the health service in Wales – and we know how badly wrong those have gone in England. And that was quite a productive time, I think, the coalition government. Of course, the discussions around the coalition, it's well documented how all of that went. I think Ieuan [Wyn Jones] as leader would have preferred to be First Minister in a coalition with the Conservatives and the Liberal Democrats. The women were not having that – not all the women – Elin and Jocelyn kept out of the discussion, but me, Leanne [Wood], Bethan [Sayed] and Nerys [Evans] were just like, "No," and in the end, Ieuan realised that he couldn't deliver his majority if the four of us sat as feminist nationalists, which is what we were going to do. Edwina would have wanted to work with me for two reasons. One was if we were to go further on Health and Care than was in the One Wales document, she would need me to bring my group along because she would need their votes to get through. Now, as it was, we were effectively moving the coalition Government closer towards Plaid's policies and further away from Labour's, so that was fine with me. But the other thing, of course, she could use us to justify to the Labour party centrally why she was doing things they didn't want her to do. So, stopping the private finance initiatives, which she, coming from a financial background, could see ten years down the road, were going to be a car crash, and politically she didn't like them anyway. She could go to Gordon Brown and say, "I'm awful sorry Gordon, it's these nasty nationalists we're in coalition with making me do it.'"

There were many in the two parties who were unhappy with the organisation of the coalition and felt that the gulf was too great, however, others were more pragmatic:

KAREN SINCLAIR

'I was one of six people in the Labour Group who were absolutely adamant against going into coalition with Plaid Cymru. I really don't believe in nationalism at all, devolution is bringing decision-making closer to the people not about separating Wales from the rest of the UK and I felt that we were almost giving it credence by going into coalition. So, I was one of six people who actually spoke against it at conference very vehemently, and to this day I still feel I was right.'

JANET RYDER

'I think it [the coalition] was very interesting. It put Plaid Cymru into power, but it was very highly contested within the Group and within the party because opinions were split – "This will wreck us ... this will give us a big advantage ..." I wasn't too happy about it and, in fact, I held the Shadow Education brief then, and Jane Davidson was taking through a new bill to do with colleges and further education, and it completely ignored special needs. And I could not stomach this Bill and I couldn't vote for it. I wasn't allowed to vote against it, so I left the Committee and resigned the portfolio. I couldn't do that. I'd rather stick to what I felt was right than do something that I thought was not going to be good. So, I resigned my portfolio and that was fine. I was quite happy with that. It's not an easy thing to do but there are times when you have to do what's right, what you feel to be right. And I'd gone round a number of colleges and some colleges were really good and some not so good and it needed a levelling off. It [the bill] needed to say, "This is what we expect you to provide and yes it's very expensive but those kids – they should have as much a chance of going [to college]." And some of the colleges were super. Some of the colleges were doing really well but some of them not so good. And it usually was the case that that was the budget that would be hit if a college were finding that they were having financial problems, and the opportunities should have been taken to stop that.'

JOYCE WATSON

'I knew it had to be a coalition when we had 25 [Assembly Members]. I suspected it would probably be with Plaid [Cymru]. I'm a realist, and I was I think fifty-two when I came in, so it didn't bother me. What would have bothered me more was walking away from the table and not having any influence. I don't think it's necessarily a bad thing if you have a coalition. I've never thought that – as long as it's a coalition that you feel comfortable with, and I was quite comfortable with that coalition.'

In 2011, Labour won thirty seats and the One Wales coalition came to an end. Labour continued as a minority Government:

ELIN JONES

'Yes, it was a shame, not for me as a person losing the ministerial job, but Plaid Cymru losing the opportunity to continue some of the elements of the work they'd begun in government. There was a bit of blaming the Government and Ieuan's [Wyn Jones] leadership, that too much of Plaid's attention had been on being in government rather than how to grow the party and make us more of an electoral machine, and take more of the praise for what they had achieved as the minority party in the Government, and that we were punished somewhat afterwards in the election that followed in 2011. And since then, of course, the occasional voice in Plaid Cymru, every now and then, says, well, perhaps being in Government isn't worth it, especially if one is a lesser partner in that Government, that it's too high a price to pay, because it's not reflected in election results. We'd always disagree with that, because there are things being achieved in government, policies that are important to Plaid Cymru, and that are important values too to Plaid Cymru. And, of course, what was really important, and something we are benefitting from today, constitutionally for Plaid Cymru, if Plaid Cymru hadn't been in government at that time, it's possible that this Senedd would be without legislative powers even by now. Because one of the conditions of working with Labour was that a referendum would be held in 2011, that would then, if won, as it was, give full legislative powers to this Senedd in the areas that have been devolved. So that was a very important legacy that Plaid Cymru achieved in those four years.'

HELEN MARY JONES

'I think some really good policy was delivered [during the One Wales coalition]. The quiet work that Jocelyn Davies did around public housing in Wales, that we could never get her to go on the radio and TV to talk about, but it began a transformation in Wales in moving back towards building council houses, in resourcing the housing associations much better. Elin did some really good things in the Environment portfolio. Of course, we had the new Language Act under Alun Ffred's leadership. We had the financial crash and then we had the pro-act and re-act schemes, that were joint between finance and economic development, and we should have made more of, that should have been more clearly balanced as a Plaid policy. And Edwina Hart and I got on with running Health and Social Services as a bit of a job share.'

KIRSTY WILLIAMS

After the 2016 Election, Kirsty was the only Liberal Democrat to keep her seat in the Assembly and, although it was a strange situation and a complicated decision, she decided to accept the role of Education Minister in Carwyn Jones's Cabinet:

'It was a bittersweet moment. To win in Brecon and Radnor was wonderful. We won with a majority of over 8,000, so it was the best result we'd ever been able to secure here, but there was no time to celebrate it because of what had happened with everybody else. There was a part of me that desperately wished that I had gone down with the rest of the team. It felt awful to be back when everyone else had lost. I felt very guilty. I had already made a decision that I would not be Leader of the [Wales] Liberal Democrats [again]. It had become a burden and it was clear to me that we needed somebody new to do that job. There then was a period of discussions and negotiations about the terms in which I would do that [accept the role of Education Minister], whether I would do it, what I wanted the Government to do, what I wanted to be able to do if I took on that role. There's a process which the Welsh Liberal Democrats have to go through, which includes a vote of all members to allow me to do that job. There then had to be a special conference and a vote of every single party member who wanted could turn up and vote and decide whether I could take that job in the Cabinet or not. In the end the party voted to allow me to take up thc job. When it comes down to it, I'm a Liberal Democrat and I have to abide by the rules of the party. If they'd said no, I would have respected that decision. I'm really glad they said yes. It's been a real privilege to be able to serve as a Minister in a Welsh Government even though it's in slightly strange circumstances.'

* * *

Chapter Fourteen

VOTING AT SIXTEEN

Lowering the voting age to sixteen has been a hot topic for many politicians in the National Assembly for Wales and then the Senedd, over the years.

ELUNED MORGAN

'I've done a lot of work on this, even when I was in the House of Lords, when I worked on the issue, during the Brexit Referendum. Sixteen- and seventeen-year-olds should have had the opportunity to vote then, and it could have made a difference to the vote. But what we've seen, and what the evidence has shown us, is that if people become involved in politics and start to vote at a young age, they are more likely to carry on voting. And especially too, when they are sixteen and seventeen, a lot of them are still at home, where, after eighteen, they have moved away from their communities, they don't feel as much a part of their communities. They don't feel as much for their communities, they don't feel they have as much of a stake in their communities for some years until they settle down. So, getting people into the habit of voting is really important, and earlier. We are teaching them about politics now in schools, so that is all in place. And also, people say, "Well, they don't have enough experience, they don't have enough knowledge." Everyone has knowledge now. You can go on Google. They have more knowledge, possibly, than older people who don't have that access.'

ELIN JONES

Elin was key in the battle to lower the voting age in the Welsh Parliament: 'I was very keen, when I became Llywydd, to bring about change, as well as just being Llywydd and leading and chairing Senedd meetings. I wanted to make something of that role. So, very early on, I established a commission to look at our voting system regarding how many members to elect, what voting system should be used, and also what the voting age should be. Laura McAllister led on that. She made suggestions as a commission that recommended more members, to change the voting system to STV [Single Transferrable Vote] and to then lower the voting age. There was no consensus on the first two points in the last Senedd. Not enough people supported changing the voting system and increasing numbers, so I had to focus on where there was consensus, namely, to lower the voting age. So, I introduced the legislation that went through the Senedd to lower the voting age to sixteen and seventeen, and I was very proud to do that. And I see, looking back on my period as Llywydd, as a period that perhaps invigorated young people in politics in Wales. Not everyone, of course, there is still a lot of work to do on that.'

In January 2020, legislation was passed with a majority to lower the voting age to sixteen for local elections and Welsh Parliament elections. In May 2021, young people over sixteen got the chance to vote for their Parliamentary candidates for the first time:

JULIE MORGAN

'I think it's very important. Numerically, the numbers are not huge but it's so important, I think, to show your confidence in young people and to show you respect young people and you respect their views. I had a huge amount of resistance when I introduced the bill in Westminster. People thought I was mad, "Sixteen- and seventeen-year-olds voting?" But it seems to me that quite often a sixteen-year-old would have ideas as good as a sixty-year-old. I feel that young people deserve that attention and so I think it's great. I think you are able to do things that are seen as more radical in a small body like the Assembly, and we have been able to do things here that are more difficult to do in Westminster.'

JOYCE WATSON

'I've always supported it. I think it was one of the first questions I was asked before I came in, when you do your hustings, and I said, "Yes, absolutely." I was married at sixteen, and I couldn't vote. I had people coming to my door asking for my husband, because he could vote, and I listened to the nonsense they were spouting. And I thought, "This is so unfair, because I wouldn't vote for you, but I can't do anything about it." I think it's hugely important, and I think that agendas need addressing. I'm really pleased. I know they [young people] will care about the environment, so that will drive change, and since that's something I care passionately about, that suits me. That's great. They will care about compassion as well, about a bit of kindness to each other, and mental health. We've all seen that that really needs attention and focus, and it's getting it, has been for a decade. That will be a good thing, and opportunity, because I fear now more than ever. I've done a lot with apprenticeships, the Assembly's got a good record on it. There's going to be mass unemployment with young people, and it's coming down the track very quickly. They mustn't be the lost generation, and I think the Assembly recognises that. And I think that they'll make those choices. I think what's important above all is that they get a good level of education and understanding of politics now. And that's the other thing I think we lack in the UK – educating people properly into politics, whether that's politics with a small or a big P. I would almost be sure that most people in my town don't know who their town councillors are, probably don't know who their county councillors are, and probably don't know who their Assembly Members are either. I never kidded myself that everybody knows who I am, because the facts are that only about 10 per cent of people really know who their representatives are, and probably less than that on how to get in touch with them.'

JANET RYDER

'I think this is going to be very important and I think politicians need to really get in touch with those young people because they do have a different outlook. And I think it could have a big impact on how the election goes. I think you have to start asking yourself, "What is mainstream politics? What is politics there for?" Politics is not there to support business; politics is there to produce a world that is good for people to live in. And climate change is at the heart of that, equal opportunities is at the heart of that, ensuring that everybody has a good home is at the heart of that, ensuring that everybody has a safe environment to grow up in is at the heart of that. And [for] a lot of young people – that tunes in to what they think. I think for politicians, they've got to start seriously taking trips into school, if nothing else, and just talking to fifth forms, talking to sixth forms, going to actually meet young people's groups. Politicians at election times, will spend ages going round care homes and places like that, but just look at where the real vote is going to be and get to know those young people. Just because they think differently doesn't mean it's not right, doesn't mean it hasn't got an impact. And a lot of them are quite concerned with things like the council putting a bus stop in the middle of a cycle path that they've just put round the town, and they can't understand a council that could do that, quite rightly too. Not many other people can – speaking about a local issue – but if you start listening to some of the things that come through the Youth Parliament, and the work that has been done, actually it's not just a side show. You have to start taking it seriously.'

KIRSTY WILLIAMS

Kirsty, former Welsh Parliament Education Minister and architect of the new national curriculum, looks at the importance of the development from an educational viewpoint:

'What are the characteristics of the individual who'll emerge from our education system? What kind of people do we want them to be? We want them to be ethical, informed citizens, ready to play their part in Wales and the world. And you cannot achieve that purpose unless children know that they have a voice and that they have a right, but they also have a responsibility to participate in those systems, imperfect sometimes as they are. So, it is really important that children understand their rights and know how to use those rights in a democratic process. I'm delighted at the prospect of sixteen and seventeen-year-olds gaining the vote. It's long overdue. I speak to young people all the time who are incredibly passionate about issues that affect their local community or affect their nation or indeed affect the whole world. So, it is really important. And do people need role models? Absolutely. As somebody once said, "You can't be it unless you have seen it." And I hope that when young women look at the Assembly, and see the women in the Assembly, they can see that it's an institution they can aspire to be part of. I feel that particularly strongly as a mother of three girls. There are times when I think, "Oh my goodness me, have I managed to get this balance right? Have I created people who've been impacted negatively because of what I do?" But my girls always say to me, "No, we're really proud of what you do and that helps inspire us, to know that you have to do your own thing and you have to make your own path and the first time somebody says, *you can't do that because* … you can ignore them, and you can go and do it anyway."'

BETHAN SAYED

"The vote for sixteen-year-olds has to come with better education for our young people, and that's why they have to keep a clear view on what Kirsty Williams is doing in schools to ensure that democratic element improves. Because, for example, Gwenda Thomas, former member for Neath, went into schools in Neath and talked quite negatively about independence for Wales, obviously as someone who doesn't believe in independence. And one girl in the audience, that I knew, said to her teacher, "I want Bethan to come in, to give the opposite [side]." And after I'd written in, the teacher said "No!" There was no welcome to me to go in and give the counter argument. We, as smaller parties, still have this problem in Labour areas, of going in to talk to young people. I believe, with the age going down, it will be easier for us to go in, and there will be more focus on the importance of politicians going into schools to discuss, not just the mechanics of politics but, "Why do you want to vote? What is your ideology? What is your core?" Schools at the moment are afraid to talk about why we vote, as if we are going to tell them [the pupils] to vote for us! That's not the intention, only that they know why they want to vote. I'm excited about that because a lot of young people have different opinions, perhaps, from people of fifty and sixty.'

VERONICA GERMAN

'I think it's good that they should be voting. I think there's a lot of work to be done. I did some work when I was in the Assembly about young people and them voting and, strangely enough, if you went out to schools and talked to people, a lot of them would say they shouldn't have the vote. A lot of young people would say, "We don't know anything, we're not ready for it." One of the things I think should happen more is that we should get more education, actually about policy differences between parties in schools. We shouldn't be frightened of being party-political in schools. We shouldn't be frightened about saying, "This is what Liberal Democrats stand for, this is what Plaid [Cymru] stands for, this is what Labour stands for." Of course, teachers don't want to touch it, so they should have people come in. They do around election time, but you need it all the time, this kind of sense of civic responsibility. I know, at the moment, most young people are on issue politics, they're passionate about the environment, that they have things that they are really excited about. But they don't link that with party politics and that's the missing link, if you like.'

Youth Parliament

In October 2016, members of the National Assembly voted to establish a dedicated Youth Parliament. Around 5000 young people throughout Wales were consulted to determine the aim and objectives, work and membership of the brand new Senedd. Members of the first Youth Parliament were elected in December 2018:

BETHAN SAYED

'I lobbied straight away. I certainly raised [the issue of] young people and wanted a real Parliament for young people since I was elected [in 2007]. Because I knew that Funky Dragon[6] represented young people but it wasn't a Senedd. It wasn't a Parliament for young people. It worked with the Government more often, and it worried about being critical of the Government because of how it was funded. So, the fact that there is now a Young People's Parliament for Wales is fantastic in my opinion.'

SUE ESSEX

'I've been enormously impressed by the Youth Parliament and these other people that are starting to get involved. Yes, sixteen- and seventeen-year-olds have the right to have their voice heard. It's not just a question of voting, they have rights in all sorts of ways. I personally think they'll be an election force and politicians will have to listen to them. How far they can articulate that, I don't know. But going back to what people do in schools – what people do in their families I think [is important]. I used to organise mock elections for largely sixteen-year-olds in my secondary schools when I was there. I used to love doing that, people used to get involved, and it was remarkable the number of youngsters who didn't even discuss politics in their family. Never ever went there. There were a large number of youngsters who didn't even have the fundamentals. So, they would say things [like], "I honestly don't know who to vote for. I just see these names and I don't know what the [party] names by them mean." There is a massive hole in our education right across Britain, I think, and that needs to be addressed.'

---

6   *Funky Dragon was the Children and Young People's Assembly for Wales, a peer-led organisation that provided opportunities for young people up to the age of twenty-five to have their voices heard on issues that affected them. It ceased in 2014.*

ELIN JONES

'Young people were so angry, a lot of them, with the fact they didn't have a voice in the referendum in 2016, that at sixteen and seventeen, they didn't have a say on whether Wales should stay in the European Union or not. So, giving some sort of hope to them that Wales, within our Parliament, respected their voice, and wanted to hear that voice, establishing the Youth Parliament – young people called for this Youth Parliament, it wasn't my idea – was very important to me to see that structure being created, and even until today, I think, the meeting that I have enjoyed and had the best inspiration from, that I've ever chaired, was that first meeting of the Youth Parliament. Sixty members were there with their very varied backgrounds, and they had a different political opinion too. But somehow, they had such energy and such hope for the future of Wales and what Wales should be, it was totally inspiring for me, that first day I chaired the first Youth Parliament session. And it enlivened my hope, even in the gloom of the 2016 referendum result, that young and very capable people could ensure the future of our country.'

* * *

Chapter Fifteen

LEGACY AND RECOLLECTIONS

Looking back over twenty years, what do the members feel they have achieved by devolution and what opportunities have been missed?

ELUNED PARROTT

'I think that devolution itself, as a journey, has given Wales confidence. I took part in a concert in 1999 called Voices of a Nation, in Cardiff Bay. I used to sing in the BBC Welsh choir, and we took part in this great big concert. It was Tom Jones and Catatonia, and Shirley Bassey in one of her lovely Welsh flag dresses, and there was this outpouring of great pride in our sense of national identity. Wales experienced a part of becoming a more confident nation and I think, as the years progress, we'll see that that in itself was important. There are policy divergences between Wales and Westminster that are important in the moment, and in the time, but I think that progressive recognition of Wales's stature as a nation is probably the most important outcome over the first twenty years. If you look at policy divergence then there are ways in which we're starting to change course, particularly around the environment and trying to see the world in a slightly different way. So rather than measuring our successes and failures purely on financial terms, which is what unfortunately Westminster does when it's setting its targets, it sets them around financial impact. Being able to see more broadly, well there is an environmental impact, there is a social impact, and we can demonstrate value in different ways. There's an opportunity there for Wales to be a more holistic nation and a less avaricious nation perhaps than some of our neighbours.'

TAMSIN DUNWOODY

'We've achieved a much greater and stronger identity for Wales as a nation. I do think we've stepped out of the shadows in many ways, become far more confident in ourselves, and actually looking around having a place in the world. I think that's definitely an achievement and wouldn't have happened without the Senedd, I don't think. There are other areas that I still think we could be looking at like policing, judiciary, those are areas that we need to be exploring in the future. I think we have made impacts in our own particular areas of education and health, and we do do things differently and that's all to the good because they're all designed for what is best for the people of Wales.'

ELUNED MORGAN

'It has been a positive influence, I think, if you look at the values that the Welsh have, they are reflected in the Welsh Parliament more than they are reflected in the Westminster Parliament. That is an important thing. That is because we have had the Labour Party in power since the beginning. I think we have achieved a lot, and the thing that the Senedd should be most proud of is the Future Generations Act. I think that is something completely unique to Wales and we should be very proud of that. I think if there is somewhere where we haven't achieved, it's on the side of the economy. The economy is still weak compared to other places in Britain. We have a lot more work to do in the field of the economy and ensuring that we can give people a standard of living. We can't do that until we strengthen the economy. That's where we've missed out, I think.'

SUZY DAVIES

'From a personal viewpoint, to see a dream happen. As a member of the opposition, not many of my dreams happen often! I've seen, over the last twenty years, more people talking about being Welsh, questioning what it means to be a Welshman or a Welshwoman, questions about the language – is that part of being a Welshman or a Welshwoman? In a way, the negative things I've noticed is that people in the north and to the west saying that what is happening in Wales at the moment is repeating the mistakes of the United Kingdom, namely the voice, the power and the money is going to one part of Wales, and some still think that the political world doesn't take any notice of them. And, of course, some people still don't understand the responsibilities of the Assembly and what is devolved. Because we've had the same party in power during my period, and before, it's had an effect on people who ask, "What's the point in voting because we have the same party in power for years and years?" People in Wales have lost the chance to see how things could be different through choosing a different party to be in power for a while. But the most disappointing thing for me is our education system, I think, because the education results have fallen over the last twenty years. I'm talking about two generations of students that now don't compare with others in the UK. I'm more than happy to see a different system in Wales – something more relevant to us – but the standards have fallen. And what that has shown is that the economy in Wales hasn't had the strength to renew. Of course, I'm a Tory and I'm bound to talk about the economy, but if we don't get that right, we'll still be looking at communities in poverty without any tools to change that.'

HANNAH BLYTHYN

'I think one of the challenges is the way in which perhaps Welsh politics are influenced by the wider economic and political situation as well. When we first had a National Assembly for Wales, I was actually still not living in Wales, and it was quite interesting watching from there [England] and seeing the positive differences that were enabled in Wales because of the National Assembly. And the challenges we had at the outset of limited powers and perhaps better finances, have gone the other way round in terms of the budget available and weight of powers. I think the challenge ahead is to make sure that we have a fairer settlement for Wales to be able to do the things that we want to do with the powers we have now and the potential powers that might come down the line in future, and for me in terms of further powers is actually thinking about what can't we do now, what things are missing, and if we had them, what could we actually do with them? So being clear about what we want those powers for is really important and that actually helps with bringing people with us and getting more people to be more engaged with the Senedd and devolved politics in Wales.'

JULIE JAMES

'I'm really glad I did it. I've really enjoyed it and I'm going to stand again. We've achieved a lot that people don't quite realise, because a lot of what we've done is preserve things that were there before, that have been destroyed by the Westminster Government across the border. It's quite difficult to get that across to people. One of the reasons we didn't have a problem in the pandemic the way they have in England is because we haven't destroyed our system of local government and our system of maintained schools, and we still have a National Health Service in Wales, whereas in England it's all dissipated to the four winds, and they've had terrible problems. They have no centralised system for anything. We centralised our PPE distribution and within three weeks of the pandemic hitting, we had it all sorted, and very few people realise this, but we've been supplying PPE to England since then. We managed to reorganise this because we have the systems in place and we've preserved a lot of things that I cherish, that I hope will continue. We still have a comprehensive system of education, we have the Foundation Phase which is amazing, and we've got the kids just coming through now who've been through the whole of their lives through the Foundation scheme and you can see the difference – their levels of attainment and the gap narrowing between rich and poor children. So, I'm really proud of the way we've been able to support all of that. The things we missed? In the original Objective One funding and the European funding, we missed the nation-building things that we should have done. We should have upgraded the Heart of Wales line so had a rapid trainline through the middle of Wales to connect the north to the south, but I think we were a bit timid. And the Assembly didn't really have the power to do [these things] at the beginning. Those were lost opportunities, I think. We can make those good. We can start doing them now. But that was a little bit of a missed opportunity, it seems to me, to pull Wales together as a country.'

JANET RYDER

'I think a lot of time has been wasted in the Assembly, talking politics, and the politics has been dressed up in either opposition for or support for policies. I think it has missed a number of opportunities to move away from what was perceived as the traditional three-party system, and I think that's a shame. You have a much more reflective Chamber because of the proportional representation, a Chamber that much more represents how the country feels. The country is mixed, and you have to give everybody a voice within that. And I think to some extent the Assembly has very much still split along party lines, until of late, when people have come together. And I think people value that coming together – the electorate value seeing politicians being able to work together. They appreciate having different voices, they appreciate having different points of view, but when it becomes very confrontational, they don't like it. For many people, like me, we were sold the Assembly on the point that it would be consensual and not confrontational. So, I think that it did miss the mark a little bit, that it has become more confrontational, more traditionally party based. It had the opportunity to do a lot more. But I think regional members in particular have made it work better because it takes you away from strongly constituency-based politics so that you're looking at the well-being of a whole region rather than the well-being of just one particular area of it. And I think that's a voice that needed to be heard. For me I would like to see the whole Assembly moving to a proportional representation. You could have a male and a female list in each constituency. You'd have the number of members that you need, and a gender balanced Chamber, and that would make a difference. There wouldn't be the competition between the sexes because it would be a natural thing and the two halves would come together and play their part. There must be ways to change the electoral system to make it more equal in the future as long as politicians take the work that has happened over the last couple of months, and realise you can get to a better place, despite different points of view, but you don't just oppose a policy because it's not your policy. You've got to step over that, step up to the mark and say, actually, this is the best thing for Wales, so let's all support it.'

HELEN MARY JONES

'The biggest missed opportunity is – and we're talking about the institution as a whole and devolution as a whole – is we had such an opportunity with that investment of European money. That should have transformed our economy. There should not be children in this country living in absolute poverty. And a lot of that was wasted, a lot of that was spent on a load of bureaucratic nonsense. And what we should have been using it on, instead of endless infrastructure, is we should have been using it to build our human capital, which is what they did in the Republic of Ireland. But of course, that's against the rules. You're not allowed to spend European structural fund money on education, but this did not stop the Irish doing it, nor parts of Italy either. And I think one of the reasons why we reached the point why the people of Wales who had had so much money from Europe voted against staying as part of the European community was partly perhaps because they didn't understand, but also because the investment made didn't change people's lives. We have a higher percentage of our children living in poverty now than we did in 1999. So that's the biggest lost opportunity. But I think there are things to be really proud of. I think what this institution has done around the rights of children, enshrining the UN Convention of the Rights of the Child in Law, the establishment of the Children's Commissioner's office, that clear voice that children are citizens in their own right. I campaigned very hard when I was with Youth Cymru, when I was out of the Senedd, for the establishment of the Youth Parliament, and that's been really great to see. And the way that the young people are interacting now with the adult Assembly and actually putting things on our agenda and challenging us on committees. And next week, we will give our children equal protection under the law with adults [Children (Abolition of Defence of Reasonable Punishment) (Wales) Act 2020] and that would not be happening without devolution.'

ANTOINETTE SANDBACH

'I'm sure lots of opportunities have been missed. I referred to one earlier with the baby loss legislation, and I think a lot more can be done for rural communities in Wales that remain taken for granted. But I think there have been achievements, and I think the Assembly has very often led the way. It led the way on the plastic bag legislation. I think the Assembly can be a bit lighter of foot and it can be quite radical and forward-thinking, which you've seen with the Future Generations Bill. But it's not as open, it's too tribal, and that I see as a problem. It's not open to things really being improved in the Assembly, like proper amendments, I would argue; I don't know whether that was because I was there at the very first time it was legislating and therefore there's a process of learning about legislation. But tabling amendments, amendments being passed – I really don't think it was as good as it could be.'

JANE DAVIDSON

'I think the famous statement about the Assembly by Ron Davis, at the time when the Government of Wales Act [1999] was first passed, "This is a process not an event," is still true today. It's a very new institution. It's only in its 21st year. It's only achieving what used to be the age of majority for my parents, now. And to have ambitious legislation where it is the only legislature in the world which is supporting future generations is a massively big agenda to live up to. I generally feel proud of its journey, and I feel proud to have been part of that journey. It has sought over a period of time to create distinctive policies for Wales, but to be mindful about the fact that Wales needs to be an outward looking country, and therefore to engage people to come and live in Wales. Encourage people from Wales to go out into the world. Bringing the best of Wales to the world and the best of the world to Wales is the real way in which I hope the institution will carry on developing.'

JOCELYN DAVIES

'Of course, since a child I'd wanted a parliament for Wales, and this was something that was really important to me and to my country. It was absolutely fabulous [when the Assembly became a Senedd] and when I think back to 2007 – if we hadn't done what we did in 2007 [formed a coalition and One Wales government with the Labour Party] that wouldn't have happened. Sometimes, when you do something now it means that in the future something else could happen. I have certainly noticed that there is more of a confidence in Welsh Labour too about their Welshness and I think that's fabulous. Where will that lead in the future? Well, we'll see. Taking back those powers [in 2007] meant that we had coalition, and coalitions have led to us having a Parliament. Otherwise, we would have all been deflated unless that Assembly could have grown into an institution, we could be proud of, and the Welsh Nation has got confidence in that institution now. I hope that the contribution that I made has made a difference. The referendum, and it now being a Parliament, which – when I think back – is why my parents joined Plaid Cymru, because they thought Wales should have its own Parliament.'

DELYTH EVANS

'I've always liked the story about Henry Kissinger going to speak with the Chinese Prime Minister, Zhou Enlai, in the '70s, and Kissinger knew that Zhou Enlai had an interest in European history. Kissinger asked Zhou Enlai what he thought about the effect of the French Revolution on European civilisation, and Zhou Enlai's answer was, "It's too early for us to know the effect." And I think that's true of the Assembly. The Assembly has been here for twenty years. It has done a lot of good things. It hasn't done well enough on some levels, but it is doing good work. But I think the good work and the effects are going to be better in the future. And some of the most important policies are happening now, starting to have an effect now – the new curriculum, for example. We lost the first ten years of the Assembly through not paying enough attention to education. I think that has been a failure. But good work is happening now and I'm proud of that and hope the new curriculum will be a success. But that's going to take a while to work its way through. The One Million [Welsh] Speakers policy is incredibly important but work is only just beginning on that. The Well-being of Future Generations Act – we'll see. That is very ambitious, that is going to take time to have an effect, but it could be particularly influential on our communities in Wales. And then the work that is happening on the base economy – very important, but that is something very new. So, I'm hopeful for the future and think we'll see more progress in the years to come. And I think this first period, twenty years, it sounds like a very long time but in the history of a nation, it's an incredibly short time.'

* * *

Appendix 1

INDEX OF MEMBERS

Female Members of the Welsh Assembly – Senedd Cymru / Parliament for Wales 1999–2021 interviewed during the project

Lorraine Barrett, Welsh Labour, Cardiff South and Penarth, 1999–2011 (interview under embargo until March 2030)

Hannah Blythyn, Welsh Labour, Delyn, 2016–current

Dawn Bowden, Welsh Labour, Merthyr Tydfil and Rhymney, 2016–current

Michelle Brown, Former UKIP / Now Independent, North Wales, 2016–2021

Jayne Bryant, Welsh Labour, Newport West, 2016–current

Eleanor Burnham, Welsh Liberal Democrats, North Wales, 2001–2011

Angela Burns, Welsh Conservatives, Carmarthen West and South Pembrokeshire, 2007–2021

Christine Chapman, Welsh Labour, Cynon Valley, 1999–2016

Jane Davidson, Welsh Labour, Pontypridd, 1999–2011

Janet Davies, Plaid Cymru, South Wales West, 1999–2007

Jocelyn Davies, Plaid Cymru, South Wales East, 1999–2016

Suzy Davies, Welsh Conservatives, South Wales West, 2011–2021

Tamsin Dunwoody, Welsh Labour, Preseli Pembrokeshire, 2003–2007

Sue Essex, Welsh Labour, Cardiff North, 1999–2007

Delyth Evans, Welsh Labour, Mid and West Wales, 2000–2003

Nerys Evans, Plaid Cymru, Mid and West Wales, 2007–2011

Janet Finch-Saunders, Welsh Conservatives, Aberconwy, 2011–current
(interview under embargo until October 2030)

Lisa Francis, Welsh Conservatives, Mid and West Wales, 2003–2007

Veronica German, Welsh Liberal Democrats, South Wales East, 2010–2011

Janice Gregory, Welsh Labour, Ogmore, 1999–2016

Lesley Griffiths, Welsh Labour, Wrexham, 2007–current

Siân Gwenllian, Plaid Cymru, Arfon, 2016–current

Edwina Hart, Welsh Labour, Gower, 1999–2016

Vikki Howells, Welsh Labour, Cynon Valley, 2016–current

Jane Hutt, Welsh Labour, Vale of Glamorgan, 1999–current

Julie James, Welsh Labour, Swansea West, 2011–current

Pauline Jarman, Plaid Cymru, South Wales Central, 1999–2003

Delyth Jewell, Plaid Cymru, South Wales East, 2019–current

Ann Jones, Welsh Labour, Vale of Clwyd, 1999–2021

Elin Jones, Plaid Cymru, Ceredigion, 1999–current

Helen Mary Jones, Plaid Cymru, Llanelli seat 1999–2003; 2007–2011; Mid
and West Wales 2003–2007; 2018–2021

Laura Anne Jones, Welsh Conservatives, South Wales East, 2003–2007, 2020–current

Baroness Eluned Morgan, Welsh Labour, Mid and West Wales, 2016–current

Julie Morgan, Welsh Labour, Cardiff North, 2011–current

Lynne Neagle, Welsh Labour, Torfaen, 1999–current

Eluned Parrott, Welsh Liberal Democrats, South Wales Central, 2011–2016

Rhianon Passmore, Welsh Labour, Islwyn, 2016–current

Baroness Jenny Randerson, Welsh Liberal Democrats, Cardiff Central, 1999–2011

Jenny Rathbone, Welsh Labour, Cardiff Central, 2011–current

Janet Ryder, Plaid Cymru, North Wales, 1999–2011

Antoinette Sandbach, Welsh Conservatives, North Wales, 2011–2015

Bethan Sayed, Plaid Cymru, South Wales West, 2007–2021

Karen Sinclair, Welsh Labour, Clwyd South, 1999–2011

Catherine Thomas, Welsh Labour, Llanelli, 2003–2007

Gwenda Thomas, Welsh Labour, Neath, 1999–2016

Joyce Watson, Welsh Labour, Mid and West Wales, 2007–current

Kirsty Williams, Welsh Liberal Democrats, Brecon and Radnorshire, 1999–2021

Leanne Wood, Plaid Cymru, South Wales Central 2003–2016; Rhondda, 2016–2021

Appendix 2

BIOGRAPHIES OF MEMBERS

Lorraine Barrett, Welsh Labour, Cardiff South and Penarth, 1999–2011 (interview under embargo until March 2030). Lorraine was born in the Rhondda, the daughter of a coalminer. She worked as a nurse and for Littlewood Pools as a typist, as a councillor, and also as assistant to the then Cardiff South and Penarth Member of Parliament, Alun Michael. She was elected to the Welsh National Assembly as the member for Cardiff South and Penarth in May 1999 and was re-elected twice before declining to stand for re-election in 2011. Lorraine sat on the Education, Environment and Health Committees, and chaired the Co-operative Party Group and the All-Party Parliamentary Group on Animal Welfare within the Assembly and was the Assembly's Commissioner for a Sustainable Environment.

Hannah Blythyn, Welsh Labour, Delyn, 2016–current. Hannah was born in Chester and grew up in Flintshire. She studied English Literature at De Montfort University in Leicester, after which she worked in Westminster for Mark Tami, MP for Alyn and Deeside, and after that for a small charity in London, Student Action for Refugees, and for a union which later became Unite Trade Union, in various roles. Returning to Wales, Hannah stood for election in 2015 as the Labour Candidate for Delyn, which is the role she holds now, and was elected Assembly Member in 2016. She currently serves as Deputy Minister for Social Partnership and was previously Deputy Minister for Housing and Local Government. She is a former co-chair of LGBT+ Labour.

Dawn Bowden, Welsh Labour, Merthyr Tydfil and Rhymney, 2016–current.

Dawn was born in Bristol, England and, before her election to the Welsh Assembly, she worked as a secretary in Guest, Keen and Nettlefolds, the NHS and Bristol City Council, and was the head of health for UNISON Cymru/Wales. In the Assembly, Dawn served on the Health and Social Services Committee; the External Affairs and Additional Legislation Committee, which dealt with Brexit; Culture, Welsh Language and Communications Committee; Constitutional and Legal Affairs Committee; Climate, Environment and Rural Affairs (CERA) and currently serves on the Children, Young People and Education Committee and the Equality, Local Government and Communities Committee, and she also chaired the Committee on Senedd Reform. She has been Chief Whip of the Welsh Government and Deputy Minister for Arts and Sport since 2021.

Michelle Brown, Former UKIP / Now Independent, North Wales, 2016–2021.

Michelle was born in Warrington but was raised in Holywell and Mostyn, North Wales. She went to school locally and went to boarding school in Holywell. She obtained a Bachelor's and a Master's degree in Law and a Post Graduate Diploma in Legal Practice from Staffordshire University, and later worked as a legal advisor in the engineering sector. In the 2016 National Assembly for Wales election, Michelle was elected as a UKIP Member for North Wales. She served on the External

Affairs and Legislation Committee, Education Committee and the Petitions Committee, and in March 2018, she was chosen by the UKIP Assembly group to be their representative on the party's National Executive Committee. A year later, Michelle resigned from UKIP to become an independent AM, accusing the UKIP group of sexism. In the 2021 Senedd election, she stood for re-election as an Independent candidate on the North Wales list vote but was unsuccessful.

Jayne Bryant, Welsh Labour, Newport West, 2016–current.

Jayne was born in Newport, South Wales, and studied at Keele University, graduating with a degree in History and Politics. She did some work experience for Paul Flynn MP and, when devolution came in 1999, she got a job with Rosemary Butler in the first Assembly. Jayne was elected as the Labour AM for Newport West in 2016, and has served on the Health, Social Care and Sport Committee, the Environment and Climate Change Committee and the Rural Affairs Committee. She chairs the Standards of Conduct Committee, the Cross-Party Groups on Diabetes; Preventing Child Sexual Abuse; Arts and Health and Suicide Prevention, and acts as Vice Chair for the Cross-Party Groups on Dementia and Intergenerational Solidarity.

Eleanor Burnham, Welsh Liberal Democrats, North Wales, 2001–2011.

Eleanor was born in Wrexham and brought up in Gwnodl Fawr, Cynwyd, a fluent Welsh speaker. She went to Radbrook College, Shrewsbury, then to Manchester University and did a degree in business. Her early career was in social services management, and she was a Wrexham Magistrate and a member of Denbigh Hospital Mental Health Tribunal. She won a prize in the Soprano category at the Llangollen International Eisteddfod and is a former member of Mid Wales Opera. Eleanor succeeded as Liberal Democrat AM for North Wales in 2001 on Christine Humphreys' resignation due to of ill-health, and was the Assembly spokesperson on Culture, Welsh Language and Sport. She sat on the Education, Environment, Equality, and Pensions Committees and the Commonwealth Parliamentary Society. After losing her seat in 2011, Eleanor retrained as a teacher.

Angela Burns, Welsh Conservatives, Carmarthen West and South Pembrokeshire, 2007–2021.
Angela was born in Shaftesbury, in Dorset and brought up overseas. After leaving school, she worked for companies such as Waitrose, Thorn EMI and Asda. She later moved to Pembrokeshire with her husband and became active in politics and local issues, primarily the proposed downgrading of the Glangwili and Withybush hospitals. She was elected to the Welsh Assembly in 2007 and served as Shadow Minister for Finance and Public Sector Delivery, for Transport and Regeneration and as Shadow Education Minister and Shadow Cabinet Secretary for Health and Well-Being. Angela decided not to stand for election in 2021. She was appointed Member of the Order of the British Empire (MBE) in the 2022 Birthday Honours for political and public service.

Christine Chapman, Welsh Labour, Cynon Valley, 1999–2016.
Christine was born in Porth, Rhondda, and was one of the first intake of politicians into the Assembly. During her 17 years there she represented Cynon Valley, was a Deputy Minister across a range of portfolios and chaired a number of committees including the Objective One Programme Monitoring Committee. She was one of Wales's representatives on the Committee of the Regions in Brussels. She campaigned for many years to end the physical punishment of children. The Children [Abolition of Defence of Reasonable Punishment] Bill was passed by the Senedd in 2020.

Her background was in education and she had served as an elected member of Rhondda Cynon Taf County Borough Council. She holds degrees from Aberystwyth, and Cardiff Universities and obtained her doctorate from the University of South Wales in 2016. She was formerly Chair of Women's Archive Wales.

Jane Davidson, Welsh Labour, Pontypridd, 1999–2011.

Jane was born in Birmingham but brought up in the United States and Zimbabwe, where she went to school, and later studied at Malvern Girls College, a boarding school. She completed a degree in English literature at Birmingham and, after graduating, she moved to Lampeter, where she did an intensive Welsh course. Her first job was teaching English, PE and drama in Cardigan High School. She also worked as a youth leader before entering politics. Following election to the Assembly, Jane served as Minister for Education and Lifelong Learning and as Minister for the Environment, Sustainability and Housing in the Welsh Government, and was instrumental in driving forward the agenda that led to the passing of the Well-being and Future Generations Act in 2015. She didn't seek re-election to the Assembly in 2011 and, after her move to live on a small holding in West Wales, took up employment as director of the Wales Institute for Sustainability at the University of Wales Trinity St David, where she is now Emeritus Pro-Vice Chancellor.

Janet Davies, Plaid Cymru, South Wales West, 1999–2007.

Janet was born in Cardiff and was brought up in Llanharry. She was educated at Howell's School Llandaff, Cardiff, and Trinity College, Carmarthen (BA Hons), and the Open University (BA Hons), after which she worked as a nurse and midwife. A former Member of Taff Ely Borough Council, Leader of Council, 1991–96, and Mayor from 1995 to 1996, she contested the Pontypridd constituency for Plaid Cymru in the 1983 General Election, the 1985 Brecon and Radnor by-election, and Merthyr Tydfil and Rhymney in the 1987 General Election. After election to the 1999 Welsh Assembly, she was a member of the Plaid Cymru National Executive and Chief Whip for the Plaid Group. Janet was a member of the Local Government and Housing Committee and the Agriculture Committee. In the Second Assembly, she served on the Audit Committee (Chair); Scrutiny of the First Minister Committee; Public Audit Act Commencement Order Committee; Public Audit (Wales) Bill Committee.

Jocelyn Davies, Plaid Cymru, South Wales East, 1999–2016.

Jocelyn was born in Usk, brought up in Newbridge, and was educated at Newbridge Grammar School and Gwent Tertiary College. She was a councillor on Islwyn Borough Council between 1987 and 1991, and contested the 1995 Islwyn by-election. In 1997, she went to Oxford University to read Law but dropped out to take up her seat in the Assembly in 1999. Jocelyn sat on a number of committees, including the Agricultural Committee, the Post-16 Committee, the Health Committee, the Local Government Committee and the Public Accounts Committee. She chaired the Committee on the Inquiry into the E coli outbreak in Wales, the South Wales East Regional Committee, and the Finance Committee. She also served as Plaid Cymru's Business Manager and Deputy Minister for Housing and Regeneration. Jocelyn retired from the National Assembly at the 2016 election.

Suzy Davies, Welsh Conservatives, South Wales West, 2011–2021.

Suzy was born in Swansea, and grew up in Bridgend, Aberdare, Cardiff, and Brecon, and is a graduate of Exeter University and the University of Glamorgan (the University of South Wales). After a career in marketing and management, she worked as a solicitor, with vulnerable families and tax planning. She has mentored young offenders and has been a trustee of a number of children's projects and community support groups. Prior to her election as an Assembly Member in 2011, Suzy contested UK parliamentary seats twice for the Welsh Conservative Party. After being elected she was appointed as Shadow Minister for Tourism, Culture and the Welsh Language, and sat on the Constitutional & Legislative Affairs Committee as well as the Children & Young People Committee. In May 2013, she was named honorary President of Swansea Conservative Future. She was re-elected as top of the Conservative list in 2016 but was moved down the list in 2021 and lost her seat.

Tamsin Dunwoody, Welsh Labour, Preseli Pembrokeshire, 2003–2007. Tamsin was born in Totnes, Devon, and was the daughter of former Labour MPs Gwyneth Dunwoody and Dr John Dunwoody. Educated at the Grey Coat Hospital Church of England girls' school in Westminster and at the University of Kent, she then trained in the National Health Service and worked in London hospitals for several years. Tamsin was elected as Assembly Member for Preseli Pembrokeshire in 2003, and in October 2005 she became Deputy Minister for Environment, Planning and Countryside and Deputy Minister for Economic Development and Transport. In the 2007 election, she lost her seat to Conservative Party candidate Paul Davies, but was selected as the Labour candidate at the Crewe and Nantwich by-election, which was triggered by the death of her mother in 2008, losing to Conservative candidate Edward Timpson. Tamsin sought the Labour nomination for Islwyn ahead of the 2010 general election but without success.

Sue Essex, Welsh Labour, Cardiff North, 1999–2007. Sue was born in Cromford, Derbyshire, and brought up in Tottenham. Sue studied geography at Leicester and afterwards did town planning, creating communities working in a local authority, later becoming a college lecturer. She moved to South Wales in 1971 and became a member of Cardiff City Council, which she led from 1994 to 1996. She was instrumental in pushing a green agenda in the city. She was elected Labour Assembly Member for Cardiff North in the National Assembly for Wales's inaugural elections in 1999, and appointed Minister for Environment, Transport and Planning in 2000. She became the Minister for Finance, Local Government and Public Services following the 2003 election, but stood down in the 2007 election.

Delyth Evans, Welsh Labour, Mid and West Wales, 2000–2003. Delyth was born in Cardiff and attended Ysgol Gyfun Rhydfelen (near Pontypridd) and the University of Wales, Aberystwyth (BA Hons, French). After graduating, she went to London and worked for a book publishing company before doing a post-grad in the College of Journalism, Cardiff University. Following this, she worked in HTV and at the BBC before becoming an assistant to Gordon Brown MP in 1992. She was also policy adviser and speechwriter to the former Labour leader John Smith, having joined the Labour Party in 1984, and former special adviser to Alun Michael. Delyth became the Assembly Member for Mid and West Wales in May 2000 following the resignation of Alun Michael, and was appointed Deputy Minister for Rural Affairs, Culture & the Environment. She did not contest the 2003 election, but has stood in subsequent ones, unsuccessfully.

Nerys Evans, Plaid Cymru, Mid and West Wales, 2007–2011.
Nerys was born in Carmarthenshire and was educated at Ysgol Gyfun Gymraeg Bro Myrddin. She obtained a BA in Government and Political Theory from Manchester University followed by a MSc in Welsh Politics at Cardiff University. An organiser for Plaid Cymru in Carmarthen East and Dinefwr, she worked as press officer for the Plaid Cymru group on Carmarthenshire County Council. In 2007, she won the Mid and West Wales regional seat vacated by Helen Mary Jones. Nerys was on the Culture Committee and co-established sub-committees to look at broadcasting and the press in Wales. She was Plaid Cymru's Education Spokesperson from 2009 to 2011 and Chaired the Assembly Cross Party group for Broadband in rural Wales. She was the Director of Policy for Plaid Cymru and authored their 2011 Assembly Manifesto. She contested the Carmarthen West and South Pembrokeshire seat for the 2011 elections, but finished in third place, losing her seat in the Assembly.

Janet Finch-Saunders, Welsh Conservatives, Aberconwy, 2011–current (interview under embargo until October 2030). Janet was born in Accrington, grew up in Huncoat, Lancashire, moving to Wales when she was 11 years old, where her parents ran a hotel. Janet went to school in Ysgol John Bright and then to Llandrillo Technical College to study business management. She ran a chain of businesses across north Wales. Prior to her election to the Welsh Assembly, Janet previously represented the Craig-Y-Don ward on Llandudno Town Council, and Conwy County Borough Council. Janet has served as the Welsh Conservative Assembly Member for Aberconwy since 2011. and, having previously held the portfolio for Social Services, represented the Group as Shadow Minister for Local Government, 2012–2016, sitting on the Communities, Equality and Local

Government Committee, and she retains this portfolio as Shadow Spokesperson for Local Government into the Fifth Assembly. Janet is a former Mayor of Llandudno, a position held by both her parents before her.

Lisa Francis, Welsh Conservatives, Mid and West Wales, 2003–2007.
Lisa was born in London, of London-Welsh parents who had been raised in London, but in 1969, the family moved to Dinas Mawddwy in Gwynedd, where they ran a hotel, and later a hotel in Aberystwyth, where Lisa continued her education. She then did a bilingual secretarial course in London, with French as the main language, working thereafter in the Lead Industries Group Limited then the pharmaceutical company Glaxo Limited. She served on Aberystwyth's Town Council before unsuccessfully contesting Meirionnydd Nant Conwy at the 2001 General Election, and Mid and West Wales successfully in the 2003 Welsh Assembly elections. After election, she sat on the Arts and Culture Committee and on the Economic Development Committee, and was Chair of the Regional Committees for a year. In 2007, she won the Dodd's Assembly Woman of the Year Award but lost in her seat the same year.

Veronica German, Welsh Liberal Democrats, South Wales East, 2010–2011.
Veronica was born in Birmingham but has lived in the Newport and Cwmbran area for nearly 30 years. She graduated in Chemical Engineering at Aston University and obtained a Masters in Biochemical Engineering from the University of Birmingham. She later worked as a teacher and taught Science, Maths and ICT in schools in Gwent. She served as a Newport Liberal Democrat councillor before being elected as a Torfaen councillor representing Llanyrafon North in 2008. In May 2010, the then Assembly Member for South Wales East, Mike

German, her husband, was named to the House of Lords, and Veronica succeeded him as an AM, as she was the next candidate on the regional party list. She was the Welsh Liberal Democrat Spokesperson for Health, Local Government and Equality; a member of the Petitions Committee; the Equal Opportunities Committee; the Health, Wellbeing and Local Government Committee; and the Legislation Committee. She failed to retain her seat in the 2011 Assembly election and the following year did not recontest her Llanyrafon North Council seat. She contested the Monmouth Assembly constituency during the 2016 election and the same seat in the 2017 general election, being unsuccessful on both occasions.

Janice Gregory, Welsh Labour, Ogmore, 1999–2016. Janice was born in Treorchy, the daughter of Raymond Powell, Labour Party MP for Ogmore from 1979. She was educated at Bridgend Grammar School for Girls and, after training in communications and working in the local telephone exchange, she became Constituency Secretary to her father from 1991. She was Women's Officer for the CLP (Constituency Labour Party) and Chair of the Ogmore Women's Forum. In 1999, she was selected as Labour candidate for Ogmore for the election to the National Assembly for Wales. She held the seat for Labour and was appointed as Labour group whip but resigned this position in February 2000 after Alun Michael resigned as First Minister. Janice voted in favour of a building a landmark headquarters building for the Assembly. When her father suddenly died in December 2001, she declined to seek selection for his Westminster seat and was re-elected to the Welsh Assembly in the 2003, 2007 and 2011 elections. She was made Chair of the Social Justice and Regeneration Committee and was Chief Whip until her retirement in 2016.

Lesley Griffiths, Welsh Labour, Wrexham, 2007–current. Lesley was born in Scotland, but in less than three weeks her parents moved back to Wales, firstly to Saltney in Flintshire, then to Wrexham, where she has lived and worked all her adult life, including 20 years working at the Wrexham Maelor Hospital. Prior to her election, she worked as Constituency Assistant to Ian Lucas, MP, being elected to the National Assembly for Wales in May 2007. In December 2009 she was appointed Deputy Minister for Science, Innovation and Skills. Following her re-election in May 2011, she was appointed Minister for Health and Social Services. In March 2013, Lesley was appointed Minister for Local Government and Government Business. In September 2014, she was appointed Minister for Communities and Tackling Poverty and in 2016 Minister for Energy, Environment and Rural Affairs. Following her re-election in 2021, Lesley was appointed Minister for Rural Affairs and North Wales.

Siân Gwenllian, Plaid Cymru, Arfon, 2016–current. Siân was born in Dolgellau and educated at Ysgol Friars, Bangor, and at Aberystwyth and Cardiff Universities. She has been a passionate campaigner for women's equality and the Welsh language for over 45 years. Before her election to the Assembly, Siân worked as a journalist with the BBC, HTV and *Golwg*, and in public relations including as press officer for Gwynedd Council. Between 2008 and 2016 she served as a councillor on Gwynedd Council, representing the village where she grew up, Y Felinheli. Between 2010 and 2014, she was responsible for the authority's finance portfolio, a member of the Cabinet for Education, Children and Young People, and Deputy Leader of the Council. In 2014 Siân was appointed as Gwynedd's small business champion, responsible for promoting this sector of the economy in the county. Siân was re-elected to the Welsh Parliament in 2021, doubling her majority with 63.3 per cent of the vote – the highest percentage of any Member of the Welsh Parliament.

Edwina Hart, Welsh Labour, Gower, 1999–2016.

Edwina was born and raised in Gowerton, Swansea, and was the first female president of the banking union BIFU (Banking, Insurance and Finance Union) now part of Unite, and went on to chair the Wales TUC (Trades Union Congress). Edwina has served as a member of the Broadcasting Council for Wales, the Wales Millennium Centre, the Employment Appeal Tribunal and the South Wales West Economic Forum. She was also a non-executive director of 'Chwarae Teg' – an organisation which promoted the role of women in the workplace. Edwina was awarded an MBE in 1998 for services to the trade union movement. Edwina served as the Assembly's first Finance Secretary, and in 2000 the role was changed to include responsibility for local government, so she became Minister for Finance and Local Government. After the 2003 Assembly election, Edwina was appointed the Social Justice and Regeneration Minister and was appointed to Health and Social Services in May 2007. Following her re-election in May 2011, Edwina was appointed Minister for Business, Enterprise and Technology, but stood down in the 2016 Welsh Assembly elections.

Vikki Howells, Welsh Labour, Cynon Valley, 2016–current.

Vikki was born in Aberdare and raised in Cwmbach, where she lived until she went to university. She attended St John's Church School in Aberdare before going to Cardiff University to do a degree in International and Welsh History, doing a Masters there as well, looking at the South Wales Valleys during the industrial revolution. Whilst studying at Cardiff, Vikki received the Charles Morgan award in recognition of her contribution to the field of

Welsh History. Vikki worked as a history teacher at St Cenydd Community School, Caerphilly, from 2000 to 2016, where she also undertook a range of pastoral roles, most recently serving as Assistant Head of Sixth Form. Vikki has also worked as a mentor for trainee teachers and has sat on the admissions panel for the History PGCE course at the University of Wales Trinity Saint David. Vikki joined the Labour Party at the age of seventeen and has undertaken many roles within her Constituency, including Women's Officer and CLP Chair. Vikki was elected to Chair the Welsh Labour Group of Assembly Members in November 2017.

Jane Hutt, Welsh Labour, Vale of Glamorgan, 1999–current.

Jane Hutt spent part of her childhood in Uganda and Kenya, and was educated at the University of Kent, the London School of Economics and Bristol University. She has lived and worked in Wales since 1972. Jane became the first National Co-ordinator of Welsh Women's Aid in 1978 and was a founder of South Glamorgan Women's Workshop. She went on to become the first director of the Tenant Participation Advisory Service (TPAS Wales) and was subsequently director of Chwarae Teg (Fair Play). Jane was an elected member of the former South Glamorgan County Council for twelve years. She was first elected to the Assembly in 1999. Between 1999 and 2005 she served as Minister for Health and Social Services in the Welsh Government. From 2005 to 2007, she was Minister for Assembly Business and Chief Whip. In the first Cabinet of the Third Assembly, she was appointed Minister for Budget and Assembly Business. In the coalition Cabinet announced on 19 July 2007 she became Minister for Children, Education, Lifelong Learning and Skills. In December 2009 she was appointed Minister for Business and Budget, subsequently Minister for Finance until 2016 when she was appointed Leader of the House and Chief Whip at the start of the Fifth Assembly.

Julie James, Welsh Labour, Swansea West, 2011–current.
Julie was born in Swansea but spent significant portions of her youth living around the world with her family. She studied American Studies & History at University of Sussex and then law at the Polytechnic of Central London, graduating in 1982. She went on to the Inns of Court School of Law in London to train as a barrister and spent most of her legal career in local government in London before returning to Swansea to work for West Glamorgan County Council and then the City and County of Swansea. Following her election as Assembly Member representing Swansea West, she sat on several committees, including the Constitutional and Legislative Affairs Committee, Enterprise and Business Committee and Environment and Sustainability Committee. In September 2014, Julie was appointed Deputy Minister for Skills and Technology and in May 2016, she was re-elected as the Assembly Member for Swansea West by a higher majority than her previous term. In November 2017, Julie was promoted to the Cabinet as Leader of the House and Chief Whip, and in December 2018, following the election of Mark Drakeford to the position of leader of Welsh Labour and therefore First Minister, she was appointed Minister for Housing and Local Government. She is currently the Minister for Climate Change.

Pauline Jarman, Plaid Cymru, South Wales Central, 1999–2003. Pauline was born and brought up in a Valley community called Perthcelyn and educated at Mountain Ash Grammar School. After leaving school, she worked at AB Metals in the Import-Export Department and from there went to Frame Filters and similar export-import work. She married and started a family but went back to work part time. In 1976, Pauline was elected to Cynon Valley Borough Council, being appointed Mayor in 1987-8, and served until 1996, when it became Rhondda Cynon Taf.

In 1981, she was elected to Mid Glamorgan County Council and served both concurrently through to 1995-6. In 1999, Pauline was re-elected to Rhondda Cynon Taf Council and Plaid Cymru took control of it from Labour, and she became the Leader of Rhondda Cynon Taf Council. She was also elected Assembly Member for South Wales Central in 1999 and during her time at the Assembly, served on the Education Committee and the Legislation Committee. She decided to stand down in the 2003 election.

Delyth Jewell, Plaid Cymru, South Wales East, 2019–current.

Delyth was born in Caerphilly, grew up in Ystrad Mynach, and went to school in Ysgol Gyfun Cwm Rhymni, before going on to study at the University of Oxford, where she graduated with a Degree in English Language and Literature and a Masters in Celtic Studies. After graduating from university, Delyth worked as a researcher and speechwriter for the Plaid Cymru Members of Parliament in Westminster under the leadership of Elfyn Llwyd MP. In 2014, she won the Researcher of the Year Award for her work in paving the way for legislation on stalking and domestic violence. She later worked for Citizens' Advice and Action Aid. In 2019, Delyth was sworn in as the Plaid Cymru Assembly Member for South Wales East, following the death of Steffan Lewis, and she was named her party's spokesperson on Brexit and External Affairs. In 2021, Delyth was re-elected as a Member of the Senedd for South Wales East, and has been appointed her party's spokesperson on climate change, transport and energy.

Ann Jones, Welsh Labour, Vale of Clwyd, 1999–2021.

Ann Jones was born and brought up in Rhyl on the North Wales coast, where she has lived all her life. She worked for nearly 30 years in fire control rooms in North Wales and Merseyside until her election to the National Assembly for Wales in 1999. Before being elected to the Assembly, Ann served as a Rhyl Town Councillor and was the town's Mayor in 1996/7. She was also a Denbighshire County Councillor. An active trade unionist, Ann served as a national official in the Fire Brigades Union for a number of years and sat on both the Welsh Labour Party and Wales TUC Executives. In 2007, Ann announced her intention to introduce legislation to make it mandatory to install a fire suppression system in new homes. Ann chaired several Assembly Committees including the Children, Young People and Education Committee, the All Party Group on Deaf Issues, and Communities, Equality and Local Government Committee. In 2016 she was elected Deputy Presiding Officer of the National Assembly. Ann was appointed Officer of the Order of the British Empire (OBE) in the 2021 New Year Honours for parliamentary and public service in Wales.

Elin Jones, Plaid Cymru, Ceredigion, 1999–current.

Elin grew up on a farm near Lampeter, and attended Llanwnnen Primary School and Lampeter Secondary School. After receiving a BSc in Economics from the University of Cardiff, she was awarded an MSc in Rural Economics from the University of Aberystwyth. She has worked as Economic Development Officer for the Rural Wales Development Board. She has also been a director with Radio Ceredigion and the television production company Wes Glei Ltd. Elin was a member of Aberystwyth Town Council from 1992 until 1999 and she was the youngest Mayor of Aberystwyth during the 1997-98 term. Elin was National Chair of Plaid Cymru between 2000 and 2002. She was elected to the Assembly in May 1999 and, in the first term of the Assembly, was Shadow Minister for Economic Development. Following the Assembly election in 2003, she managed this portfolio until 2006, when she became Shadow Minister for the Environment, Planning and Countryside. On 9 July 2007, the One Wales Government was formed and Elin was appointed Minister for Rural Affairs. In 2009, Elin won the *Farmers Weekly* British Farming Champion award in addition to the Assembly Member of the Year award. She has served as Llywydd of the Assembly/Senedd since 2016.

Helen Mary Jones, Plaid Cymru, Llanelli seat 1999–2003; 2007–2011; Mid and West Wales 2003–2007; 2018–2021.

Helen Mary was born in Colchester, Essex, and educated at Colchester County High School for Girls, Caereinion High School in Powys and the University of Wales, Aberystwyth, where she was awarded an honours degree in history and a Postgraduate Certificate in Education. She has taught in the special education field and has held various positions in youth, community and social work. In 1999 she was elected to the new National Assembly for Wales for the constituency of Llanelli, serving as Shadow Minister for Education and Lifelong Learning, and on the committees for Education and Lifelong Learning Committee, Equality of Opportunity, and the South West Wales Regional Committee. She stood in the 2000 and 2003 Plaid Cymru leadership elections, losing to Ieuan Wyn Jones both times. In the 2003 Assembly elections, she lost her constituency seat in Llanelli by just 21 votes, but was elected for the Mid and West Wales 'top-up' region. She was the Shadow Minister for the Environment, Planning and Countryside in the Second Assembly. During the 2007 elections, she won back the Llanelli constituency but lost her seat to Labour's Keith Davies by 80 votes in the 2011 election. She was elected National Chair of Plaid Cymru in September 2011, and two months later, was appointed Chief Executive of Youth Cymru, holding this position until September 2017. In the 2016 National Assembly for Wales election, Helen Mary lost to the Labour candidate Lee Waters but returned to the Assembly in August 2018 to represent Mid and West Wales following the resignation of Simon Thomas. At the 2021 Senedd election, she was Plaid's second candidate on the list vote for the Mid and West Wales region but failed to gain a seat.

Laura Anne Jones, Welsh Conservatives, South Wales East, 2003–2007; 2020–current.

Laura was born in Newport Gwent Hospital and brought up in Usk, Monmouthshire, where she worked on the family farm. She attended the University of Plymouth, where she studied politics. She joined the Conservatives in 1996 and was involved in Conservative Future, the party's youth wing. Elected to the Assembly at the 2003 election to represent South Wales East, she was the youngest member of the Assembly. She was appointed as the Conservative spokeswoman on sport, and sat on the Culture, Sport and Welsh Language, and Local Government and Public Services committees. She lost her seat in the Assembly in the 2007 Assembly election when Plaid Cymru gained one seat in the South Wales East region at the expense of the Conservatives. At the 2015 general election she contested the Labour seat of Islwyn for the Conservatives and finished third. In the 2017 Welsh local elections she was elected to the Wyesham ward on Monmouthshire County Council winning 42 per cent of the vote. At the 2019 general election she contested the Labour seat of Blaenau Gwent for the Conservatives and finished third. Following the death of Mohammad Asghar in June 2020, it was confirmed in July 2020 that Laura would become the MS for South Wales East, having been the next Conservative candidate on the regional list in the Assembly's 2016 election. She was re-elected at the 2021 Senedd election.

Baroness Eluned Morgan, Welsh Labour, Mid and West Wales, 2016–current.

Eluned was born and brought up in Ely, Cardiff. Educated at Ysgol Gyfun Gymraeg Glantaf, she won a scholarship to the United World College of the Atlantic and gained a degree in European Studies from the University of Hull, after which she worked as a television researcher. In 1994, she was elected as a Member of the European Parliament representing Mid and West Wales, the youngest MEP when she took up her seat. She continued as an MEP representing Wales being elected at both the 1999 and 2004 elections. Eluned stood down at the 2009 European Parliament elections, after which she worked as the Director of National Development for SSE in Wales (SWALEC). In November 2010, Eluned was granted a life peerage to sit on the Labour benches of the House of Lords, and she was gazetted on 27 January 2011 as Baroness Morgan of Ely. In the 2016 Assembly elections, she was elected to the Mid and West Wales regional list, serving thereafter as Minister for Welsh Language and Lifelong Learning, the Minister for International Relations and the Welsh Language. Eluned contested the 2018 Welsh Labour leadership election, unsuccessfully, and was then appointed by First Minister Mark Drakeford as Minister for International Relations and the Welsh Language before being moved to Minister for Mental Health, Wellbeing and the Welsh Language in October 2020. She currently serves as Minister for Health and Social Services.

Julie Morgan, Welsh Labour, Cardiff North, 2011–current.

Julie was born in Cardiff and educated at Dinas Powys Primary School, Howell's School in Cardiff, King's College London, the University of Manchester and Cardiff University. She has a BA Hons in English and a postgraduate diploma in Social Administration. In 1997 Julie was elected as MP for Cardiff North, the first woman to have represented Cardiff in Westminster. She was MP for Cardiff North for thirteen years until she narrowly lost the seat by 194 votes in 2010. During her time in Westminster, she presented three Private Members' Bills – one on banning smoking in public places, one on granting votes at sixteen, and one on preventing under-eighteens from using sunbeds, which became law in 2010. Julie was elected as the Assembly Member for Cardiff North in 2011. During the Fourth Assembly she sat on the Public Accounts Committee, the Finance Committee and the Environment Committee as well as chairing seven Cross-Party Groups covering areas such as children, cancer, and nursing and midwifery. In the Fifth Assembly Julie was re-elected with the highest number of votes cast for any AM. She chaired the Cross-Party Groups on Cancer, the PCS Union and the Gypsy, Roma, Traveller CPG until becoming Deputy Minister for Health in December 2018. She was also a member of two committees, the Health, Social Care and Sport Committee and the Children, Young People and Education Committee, and is currently Deputy Minister for Social Services.

Lynne Neagle, Welsh Labour, Torfaen, 1999–current.

Lynne was born in Merthyr Tydfil in 1968 and was educated at Cyfarthfa High School, and then at Reading University, where she studied French and Italian. Before her election to the then National Assembly in 1999, Lynne held a number of posts within the voluntary sector in Wales, working for organisations such as Shelter Cymru, Mind and the CAB. She was Carers Development Officer with Voluntary Action Cardiff and also worked as a researcher for Glenys Kinnock MEP. Lynne was a long-serving chair of the Labour Group in the Assembly until 2008. Her political interests include health, housing, social services, Europe and the future of the valleys in south Wales. In the Fifth Assembly, Lynne was chair of the Children, Young People and Education Committee. She currently serves as Deputy Minister for Mental Health and Wellbeing.

Eluned Parrott, Welsh Liberal Democrats, South Wales Central, 2011–2016. Eluned was born in Abergavenny. After studying at St Peter's Collegiate School, in Wolverhampton, she gained a degree in music from Cardiff University and a postgraduate diploma in marketing from the Chartered Institute of Marketing. Before becoming an AM, she worked as a community engagement manager for Cardiff University. Eluned contested the Vale of Glamorgan seat for the Welsh Liberal Democrats at the 2010 general election. In a seat not known for Welsh Liberal Democrat successes, she polled 15.2 per cent of the vote, the highest Welsh Liberal Democrat vote share there for decades. In 2011, Eluned was elected as Assembly Member for the South Wales Central Region after John Dixon's suspension. She took on the Enterprise, Transport, Europe and Business portfolios and sat on the Enterprise and Business Committee and Constitutional and Legislative Affairs Committee.

Rhianon Passmore, Welsh Labour, Islwyn, 2016–current. Rhianon was born and educated in Islwyn and attended the Welsh College of Music and Drama. She is a champion of music and the creative arts, with a strong interest in music education and arts development. Prior to her career in politics, Rhianon was a clarinetist and a member of different orchestras. She has served on the BBC Broadcasting Council Wales and the executive body of the National Books Council for Wales. She has been very involved with her local community, setting up a number of organisations and winning some awards, including being a finalist in the Welsh Women of the Year Awards. Rhianon is a former Cabinet Member for Education at Caerphilly County Borough Council, Chair of the Education Achievement Service for South East Wales and Vice Chair of ESIS (Education Support Inclusion Services South East Wales). In July 2015, she was selected as the Welsh Labour candidate for the Islwyn constituency, and in May 2016, she was elected a Member of the Welsh Assembly. She had previously stood as a regional candidate for Mid and West Wales in the 2003 Welsh elections and a regional candidate for South Wales East in the 2007 elections, without success.

Baroness Jenny Randerson, Welsh Liberal Democrats, Cardiff Central, 1999–2011.

Jenny was born in Paddington and was educated at Bedford College, University of London, gaining a BSc in Physiology and Biochemistry. She lectured at Cardiff Tertiary College and was a Cardiff councillor 1983-2000. Jenny was elected as Assembly Member for Cardiff Central at the 1999 Assembly elections beating the Labour candidate Mark Drakeford. She served as Minister for Culture, Sport and the Welsh Language in the Liberal Democrat/Labour Partnership Government from 2000 to 2003, and acted as Welsh Deputy First Minister from July 2001 to June 2002. Jenny was Health and Social Services Minister and Equal Opportunities and Finance Spokeswoman for the Welsh Liberal Democrats during the Second Assembly. She stood for the leadership of the Welsh Liberal Democrats in 2008 but was defeated by Kirsty Williams. In the third Assembly, Jenny was the Liberal Democrat spokesperson on Education, Transport and the Economy, but did not seek re-election at the 2011 Assembly elections. In 27 January 2011, she was created a life peer as Baroness Randerson, of Roath Park in the City of Cardiff, and was introduced in the House of Lords, where she sits on the Liberal Democrat benches. In September 2012, she was appointed a Parliamentary Under-Secretary of State at the Wales Office and is the first female Welsh Liberal Democrat to hold ministerial office at Westminster and the first Welsh Liberal to hold a ministerial post since Gwilym Lloyd-George in 1945.

Jenny Rathbone, Welsh Labour, Cardiff Central, 2011–current. Jenny was born in Liverpool and worked for 20 years in current affairs television, as a researcher and reporter for Granada's *World in Action*; producer of the BBC's *Money Programme*, and on R4's *Woman's Hour*. From 2002 to 2007, she was programme manager of an award-winning Sure Start programme in north London and set up two children's centres, including a national pathfinder ante-natal service offering parenting classes and breastfeeding support working alongside midwife-led clinics. Jenny was elected to the National Assembly in May 2011 after defeating the Liberal Democrats in the Cardiff Central seat. In May 2016, she increased her majority by over 2,000 per cent. Jenny sits on the Climate Change, Environment and Rural Affairs Committee and the Public Accounts Committee and has previously served on the Children and Young People's Committee and the Equality, Local Government and Communities Committee. Jenny chairs three Cross Party Groups on Food; Gypsies and Travellers; and Women's Health.

Janet Ryder, Plaid Cymru, North Wales, 1999–2011. Janet was born in Sunderland and, after leaving education, worked as teacher and youth worker. She moved with her family to Wales and became involved with voluntary and community work in Ruthin. She served as Mayor of Ruthin, on Denbighshire County Council from 1995 to 1999, and on the Plaid Cymru National Executive. Following her election to the Welsh Assembly in 1999, she was the Shadow Minister for Local Government and Communities and in 2002 she was given additional responsibility for Finance. Janet was re-elected in May 2003 and, following a Shadow Cabinet reshuffle in November that year, she became the Shadow Minister for Education and Lifelong Learning. In April 2006, this portfolio changed to Education, Lifelong Learning and Skills, including responsibilities for schools, further education and skills development, higher education, the youth service and the careers service. During the Third Assembly, she resigned that post and became chair of the Subordinate Legislation Committee which subsequently was renamed the Constitutional Affairs Committee. She was Chair of the Wales branch of the Commonwealth Parliamentary Association and of the Cross Party Group on Autism. In March 2008, Janet launched a campaign calling on the UK Government to allow national flags such as the Welsh dragon to be displayed on car number plates. She contested Clwyd South in the 2010 general election, finishing fourth but did not stand to be re-elected in the 2011 Assembly election.

Antoinette Sandbach, Welsh Conservatives, North Wales, 2011–2015.

Antoinette was born in Hammersmith, West London. Her paternal grandmother was a prominent landowner in North Wales, whose estates included Hafodunos near Abergele and Bryngwyn Hall near Llanfyllin. Antoinette was educated at Haileybury and Imperial Service College, and the University of Nottingham, where she studied law. She practised as a criminal barrister in London for thirteen years and was twice elected to the Bar Council in that time. She then ran the family farming business, Hafodunos Farms Ltd, at Llangernyw from where she embarked on a political career. In the 2007 Welsh Assembly election, she unsuccessfully contested the Labour-held constituency of Delyn. Antoinette contested the Delyn parliamentary constituency again in the 2010 general election, but lost again. Following the death of Brynle Williams in 2011, she became a Conservative Regional Assembly Member for North Wales. During her time in the Assembly, she was appointed Shadow Rural Affairs Minister, and in 2014, Shadow Minister for the Environment. She also sat on the Assembly's Environment and Sustainability Committee. In 2015,

Antoinette was selected as the Conservative Party candidate for the Conservative-held seat of Eddisbury in Cheshire, England, and she resigned from the Welsh Assembly, to be succeeded by Janet Haworth. She held her seat in the House of Commons until 2019 when, standing as a Liberal Democrat, she lost her seat to the Conservative candidate, Edward Timpson.

Bethan Sayed, Plaid Cymru, South Wales West, 2007–2021.

Bethan was born in Aberdare, the daughter of poet Mike Jenkins. She grew up in Merthyr Tydfil, where both her parents were involved in the anti-apartheid movement of the 1980s and early 1990s. She was educated at Ysgol Gyfun Rhydfelen, near Pontypridd and graduated with a BScEcon degree in International Politics and International History at the University of Wales Aberystwyth. At university, she was elected to the Guild of Students executive, and served as Guild President, as well as becoming active in a number of campaigns. After university, she moved to work in the Rhondda, in Leanne Wood's office, working half the time for her, dealing with local, social issues, and half the time for Plaid Cymru, as a Youth Officer. Bethan was selected as Plaid Cymru's lead candidate for the South Wales West Regional list and was duly elected in the subsequent election of May 2007. She was initially Child Poverty and Culture Spokesperson for the Plaid Cymru group at the National Assembly, and sat on the Communities and Culture committee, Audit committee, and the Petitions Committee. In 2012, Bethan was appointed Plaid's spokesperson for Heritage, Welsh language and Sport, and was chairperson for the Assembly's Cross Party Eating Disorder Group. In August 2020, she announced she would not be standing in the 2021 Senedd election.

Karen Sinclair, Welsh Labour, Clwyd South, 1999–2011.

Karen was born and brought up in a suburb of Wrexham, North Wales, and was educated at Grove Park Girls School. After working in the Youth Service for fourteen years, she became a Care Manager with Wrexham Social Services for clients with learning disabilities. Karen was a member of the former Glyndwr District council for seven years, preceding the local government reorganisation and served on Denbighshire County Council. After her election to the Assembly, she broke with convention by deciding to do her speeches sitting down, to avoid the aggressive stance common in Westminster, and she was also instrumental in getting Type Talk machines into the Assembly, to aid access for people with hearing difficulties and deafness. She was Chief Whip and Minister of Assembly Business, sat on the Environment and Agriculture Committee and the Legislation Committee, and chaired the URBAN II West Wrexham Regeneration Project Monitoring Committee. In October 2009, Karen announced that she would step down from her Assembly seat at the 2011 election.

Catherine Thomas, Welsh Labour, Llanelli, 2003–2007.

Catherine was born in Dafen, Llanelli, and was educated at her village school, Dafen Primary School, and then at Llanelli Girls Grammar School, after which she went to the Polytechnic of Wales and she also did a Master's Degree at Cardiff University. Her first degree was in Humanities, majoring in history, and her Masters was in Population Studies. After her initial degree, Catherine returned to Llanelli, and worked for the local authority, in the Environment Department, and she also had a column in the *Llanelli Star*, writing about the local environment. She went on to work as a Press and Public Relations Officer for the 'Keep Wales Tidy' Campaign, which took her back to Cardiff, and after that did Press and PR for her then husband, MP Wayne David. From there, she went on to work for Julie Morgan, MP for Cardiff North, as Office Manager and Political Aide. Following her election to the Assembly in 2003, representing her home constituency of Llanelli, Catherine sat on various committees including, Legislation, the Environment, Local Government, Social Justice and Regeneration, and Equality. In 2007, she lost her seat to Helen Mary Jones, when Plaid Cymru took Llanelli from Labour.

Gwenda Thomas, Welsh Labour, Neath, 1999–2016.

Gwenda was born in Gwauncaegurwen and educated at Pontardawe Grammar School. She sat the examination to get into the Civil Service, working firstly in the County Courts Division of the Lord Chancellor's Department and then in the Benefits Agency as an Executive Officer. She represented her home village as both a community and county councillor for many years and was appointed Chair of the Social Services Committee of West Glamorgan County Council and, following local government reorganisation, of Neath Port Talbot County Borough Council – becoming the first woman to chair a major committee. Gwenda was first elected to the Assembly in May 1999 and, during her career as an AM, she served as Chair of the Housing Committee, Chair of the Equality of Opportunity Committee, and chaired a review into Safeguarding Vulnerable Children in Wales, which report 'Keeping Us Safe' was published in 2006. In the Third Assembly she was appointed Deputy Minister for Health and Social Services, and in the Fourth Assembly, she held the position of Deputy Minister for Children and Social Services. Gwenda decided not to stand for election in the 2016 election. She was awarded a Doctorate by Swansea University for her work with the children's agenda and child protection, and has been accepted into the National Eisteddfod's Gorsedd of the Bards for her contribution to Social Services in Wales.

Joyce Watson, Welsh Labour, Mid and West Wales, 2007–current. Joyce was born in Hamilton, in south Lanarkshire, where her father, who served in the Royal Artillery, was based. Later they moved to Manorbier, near Tenby, and she attended schools in Manorbier, Cosheston and Cardigan. After leaving school, she ran a number of small businesses, including public houses, restaurants and retail outlets in Ceredigion, Carmarthenshire and Pembrokeshire, before returning to education as an adult, studying at Pembrokeshire College and Swansea University. Joyce served as a Pembrokeshire County Councillor from 1995-2004. Before her election to the National Assembly for Wales in 2007, she managed the Wales Women's National Coalition and was a senior member of the Wales Gender Budget Group and NHS Equality Reference Group. She has represented the Assembly/Senedd on several international bodies: the Commonwealth Parliamentary Association (CPA) Wales branch (Chair), the British-Irish Parliamentary Assembly, and the Council of Europe's Congress of the Regions. Joyce champions the International White Ribbon campaign against domestic violence and is founder of the Assembly's anti-human trafficking group. She has sat on various committees including Economy, Economic Development, Equality, Local Government and Communities, and is currently the Commissioner for Equality.

Kirsty Williams, Welsh Liberal Democrats, Brecon and Radnorshire, 1999–2021. Kirsty was born in Taunton to Welsh parents and, from the age of three, grew up in Bynea in Camarthenshire. She was educated at the village primary school and then at St Michael's School in Llanelli. She studied at Manchester University and the University of Missouri, before working at Carmarthenshire College and for a small business in Cardiff as a Marketing Executive. Kirsty was first elected to the Assembly in

May 1999. She became the leader of the Welsh Liberal Democrats in December 2008, the first female leader of any of the four main Welsh political parties, and chaired the Health and Social Services, Standards of Conduct and Sustainability Committees. Kirsty was the Labour Government's Minister for Education during the Fifth Assembly, 2016 to 2021, and was instrumental in the introduction of a new curriculum for Wales. In December 2012, she won ITV Wales's Assembly Member of the Year Award and in the Queen's Birthday Honours 2013, was appointed Commander of The Most Excellent Order of the British Empire for public and political service. Kirsty has been involved in a long-running 'More Nurses' campaign for a law requiring minimum staffing levels for nurses in Welsh hospitals and was made an honorary fellow of the Royal College of Nursing in 2016. In the elections to the Welsh Assembly on 5 May 2016, she retained her Brecon and Radnorshire seat with an increased majority, but she stood down as leader of the Welsh Liberal Democrats the day after the election. In October 2020, Kirsty announced that she would not be seeking re-election in the 2021 election.

Leanne Wood, Plaid Cymru, South Wales Central 2003–2016, Rhondda, 2016–2021.

Leanne was born in Llwynypia and brought up in the village of Penygraig. She was educated at Tonypandy Comprehensive School and the University of Glamorgan (now the University of South Wales). After joining Plaid Cymru in 1991, Leanne was elected a Councillor for the Penygraig ward on Rhondda Cynon Taf County Borough Council but did not recontest the seat in 1999. She unsuccessfully stood in both the 1997 and 2001 elections to the UK Parliament as a candidate in the Rhondda constituency. From 1997 to 2000, she worked with the Mid Glamorgan Probation Service as a probation officer and after that as a support worker for Cwm Cynon Women's

Aid. Leanne lectured in social policy at Cardiff University from 2000, and, prior to her election to the National Assembly in 2003, was Jill Evans MEP's political researcher. After her election, Leanne served as Plaid Cymru's Shadow Social Justice Minister between 2003 and 2007. She became Plaid Cymru's sustainability spokesperson from the formation of the One Wales government, a coalition between Labour and Plaid Cymru. During the 2011 referendum on extending the National Assembly for Wales's law-making powers, Leanne was Plaid Cymru's representative on the all-party 'Yes for Wales' steering group, which campaigned successfully for a 'Yes' vote. Upon becoming leader of Plaid Cymru in 2012, Leanne refused the party leader's allowance to which she was entitled. After successfully contesting the Rhondda constituency seat in 2016, and becoming leader of the opposition, she did the same again. She lost her Rhondda seat to Labour's Buffy Williams at the 2021 Senedd election.

Appendix 3

NOTES ON THE HISTORY AND GOVERNANCE OF THE ASSEMBLY/ SENEDD

The long road to Devolution and the National Assembly for Wales

To date, there have been three devolution referenda held in Wales. The first was held on March 1st 1979 to decide whether there was enough support for a Welsh assembly following the Kilbrandon Report set up by Harold Wilson's Labour government to examine the structures of the UK constitution. The report had recommended creating devolved assemblies for Wales and Scotland but the proposals were defeated in both Wales and Scotland, with only 12 per cent of the Welsh electorate voting in favour.

The second Welsh devolution referendum, a Labour UK manifesto commitment, was held on 18 September, 1997. The referendum resulted in a narrow majority in favour of devolution, leading to the passing of the Government for Wales Act 1998 and the creation of the National Assembly for Wales in 1999.

Following a healthy 'Yes' vote in the third referendum of 2011, the Assembly's primary law-making powers were enhanced.

Voting systems

As a brand new institution, the National Assembly for Wales would create its own rules and traditions. The additional member voting system was adopted, a system perceived as fairer, more proportional, representative and democratic than the old first past the post system still adhered to by the UK Government. In the National Assembly for Wales elections, each voter would cast two votes: a vote for a candidate standing in their local constituency and a further vote for candidates on a party list for a wider region made up of multiple constituencies.

Selection

In the run up to the 1997 referendum, a cross party group of Welsh women politicians from the Labour party, Plaid Cymru and the Liberal Democrats had been planning and preparing extensively and hopefully for a new political reality. The 'Yes' vote secured they seized upon an opportunity to increase the numbers of women standing for election, by arguing for radical changes in the selection process with their respective parties.

The Labour party women were intent on a system of 'Twinning'. Under this system, two adjacent Constituency Parties would pick a woman in one constituency and a man in the other as a way of balancing selection. The Plaid Cymru women knowing that they would win fewer constituency seats than Labour fought to place women at the top of their party's list of regional top-up candidates in an attempt to seriously enhance the chances of women being elected.

After much discussion and despite serious disagreement between members, the women in both parties prevailed. The First Assembly saw 24 women elected out of the 60 members and in the 2003 election for the Second Assembly these two systems helped to ensure parity, when an equal number of male and female AMs were elected. This resulted in the National Assembly for Wales becoming a democratic national body with one of the highest proportions of women representatives and the institution was lauded as a model of gender equality worldwide.

The evolution of Welsh Devolution

The First Assembly in 1999 was frustratingly toothless as it had no powers to pass primary legislation. In July 2002, however, Welsh Government established the independent Richard Commission, with Lord Richard as Chair, to review the institution's powers and electoral arrangements and to ensure that it was able to operate in the best interests of the people of Wales. The Richard Commission reported in March 2004 and recommended that the National Assembly should have powers to legislate in certain areas, whilst others would remain the preserve of Westminster. The Commission also recommended changing the electoral system to a single transferable vote (STV) system.

A new building for Wales

The National Assembly for Wales' first home and debating chamber was based in Tŷ Crughywel, later named Tŷ Hywel after King Hywel Dda of Deheubarth, the creator of medieval Welsh Laws. The institution however quickly outgrew its first home in size and ambition. It was decided to construct the new purpose built Senedd in a nearby location to reflect the new politics of Wales. The building was designed to be as open and accessible as possible. Architects, the Richard Rogers Partnership, said: 'The building was not to be an insular, closed edifice. Rather it would be a transparent envelope, looking outwards to Cardiff Bay and beyond, making visible the inner workings of the Assembly and encouraging public participation in the democratic process.'

Construction work started in 2001 and the Senedd building was finally opened on March 1st 2006.

From Assembly to Senedd

The Assembly gained limited primary legislative powers following the 2007 election and the passage of the Government of Wales Act 2006. Following the positive result in the referendum in 2011, the Assembly's primary law-making powers were enhanced. These powers were further extended by the Wales Act 2014 and Wales Act 2017 with the latter Act moving the Assembly to a model of devolution like that of the Scottish Parliament. In May 2020, the Assembly was renamed Senedd Cymru, or the Welsh Parliament, when section 2 of the Senedd and Election (Wales) Act 2020 came into force.

Senedd reform

Since 2004, a series of reports including the 'A Parliament that Works for Wales' of 2017 (also known as the McAllister Report[7]) have recommended that the size of the Senedd should increase from its current 60 Members. The Special Purpose Committee on Senedd Reform was set up in October 2021 to come up with proposals to be included in a Welsh Government Bill to reform the Senedd. In May 2022 the First Minister, Mark Drakeford, and the then Leader of Plaid Cymru, Adam Price, published a joint statement about Senedd reform based on the proposals agreed by a majority of the Special Purpose Committee.

---

7 Professor Laura McAllister, Chair of the Expert Panel on Assembly Electoral Reform which published its report 'Parliament that Works for Wales' (also known as the McAllister Report) in December 2017. Professor Laura McAllister is a Welsh academic and an expert on devolution, Welsh politics and elections. From Bridgend, Laura is a graduate of the London School of Economics where she completed a BSc (Econ) Honours degree in Government; she later completed a PhD in Politics at Cardiff University. She was Professor of Governance at the University of Liverpool between 1998 and October 2016 and is now Professor of Governance and Public Policy at Cardiff University's Wales Governance Centre. McAllister was a member of the Richard Commission which reported in 2004 on the powers and electoral arrangements of the National Assembly for Wales. She advised the Independent Panel on AMs' Pay and Support, 2008–10 and was Chair of the Expert Panel on Assembly Electoral Reform which published its report 'Parliament that Works for Wales' (also known as the McAllister Report) in December 2017. In October 2021, she was named co-chair of the Independent Constitutional Commission on the Constitutional Future of Wales along with Dr Rowan Williams. McAllister is a former Wales football captain. She is now Vice President of UEFA and a member of its governing board, the Executive Committee, having been elected at the UEFA Congress in April 2023.

McAllister appears regularly on the BBC and other media platforms commentating on Welsh politics, elections and public policy. She also writes a regular column on current affairs, politics and sport for the *Western Mail* and Wales Online. She was the only Welsh woman to be included in the BBC's 100 Women List 2022 and was number one on the Wales Pinc List 2023.

The recommendations included:

- an increase in Senedd members from 60 to a total of 96 members.
- all members should be elected using proportional lists with integrated statutory gender quotas.
- Senedd seats should be allocated to the different parties using the D'Hondt formula, a formula used to turn votes into seats in a proportional electoral system.

First minister Mark Drakeford said: "The case for Senedd reform has been made. We now need to get on with the hard work to create a modern Senedd, which reflects the Wales we live in today. A Parliament that truly works for Wales."

.

Appendix 4

GLOSSARY

For a fuller glossary see https://senedd.wales/glossary/

All-women shortlists (AWS): positive action practice to increase the proportion of female Members of Parliament.

Backbencher: a Member of Parliament who isn't a government minister or an opposition leader.

Ballot: a system of voting, especially secret.

Bill: a proposed law. If the Senedd approves the proposals then the Bill is ready to become an Act. A Bill can only become an Act of the Senedd once it has been approved by the Monarch, a process called Royal Assent. Acts are often referred to as primary legislation.

By-election: a by-election occurs when a Senedd seat becomes vacant during a term (ie between elections) due to a constituency Member death, resignation or becomes ineligible. In the event that a regional Member is unable to sit, they are replaced by the next person on the party list.

Cabinet: The Cabinet of the Welsh Government is made up of the First Minister, Cabinet Secretaries, Ministers and the Counsel General to the Welsh Government.

Campaign: Activities held to win an election.

Candidate: a person who is competing for votes in an election.

Canvassing: a means of finding out how people will vote prior to a proposed election.

Caucus: a group of politicians with similar aims or interest.

Chair: All Senedd committees have a Chair, elected by the Senedd and who usually sits at the head of the table during committee meetings. The Chair's main role is to ensure that there is a fair balance of opportunities for committee members to ask questions and for witnesses to respond.

Chamber: This is the debating chamber in the Senedd building where Plenary Meetings of the Senedd are held. There is a public gallery above the Chamber, where members of the public can arrange to watch the meetings as they happen.

Coalition: An arrangement whereby more than one political party agrees to form a government, usually occurring where no party wins more than half the seats.

Committee: Committees are small groups of Members who collectively represent the balance of the political parties in the Senedd. One of the committee's members will have been elected by the Senedd as the committee's Chair. Committees scrutinise proposed legislation (Bills) and Welsh Government policies and make recommendations for improvements. Members who are also Cabinet Secretaries or Welsh Ministers cannot become members of committees.

Constituency: Wales is divided into 40 electoral areas, known as constituencies, and each elects a Member (MS) to the Senedd under the first-past-the-post system.

Constituency Members: The Senedd is made up of 60 elected Members. Forty are chosen to represent individual constituencies and 20 are chosen to represent the five regions of Wales.

Cross-Party Groups: Cross-Party Groups may be set up by Members in respect of any subject area relevant to the Senedd. A group must include Members from three political party groups represented within the Senedd.

Debate: a discussion between Members of the Senedd. Debates take place in the Siambr [Chamber] and can be followed by a vote.

Democracy: Democracy means that those eligible to vote can have a say in the decision-making processes. In a democratic country, elections will be held and the people choose who should represent them in a central parliament.

Devolution: Devolution is the transfer or delegation of power to a more local level. It is typically used to refer to the transfer of power from the UK's central government to the Scottish Government, Welsh Government and Northern Ireland Executive. In Wales, powers have been devolved from UK Ministers to Welsh Ministers and law-making powers from the UK Parliament to the Welsh Parliament.

Election (Wales, at present): Senedd elections are usually held every five years. The people of Wales aged sixteen or over can vote for their favoured parties and political hopefuls. Everyone that votes gets two ballot papers. One is for their Constituency Member; the person that represents their local area in the Senedd. The other is used to vote for Regional Members, but rather than voting for individuals, they vote for a political party.

Feminism: A movement for social change that aims to rid society of beliefs and traditions that stop women from having the same rights, powers and opportunities as men.

First past the post: An electoral system where the person with the highest number of votes wins. In Senedd elections, 40 Members are elected to represent constituencies using this system.

General Election: A General Election is held at least once every five years. This is when people of the UK over the age of eighteen, and who are eligible to vote have the opportunity to choose Members of Parliament (MPs) who will represent them in the UK Parliament.

Hustings: The political activities, meetings and speeches that happen prior to an election.

Independent: An elected representative who isn't a member of any political party.

Legislation: General term for new laws and the process of making them.

Legislature: A law-making body where new laws are debated and agreed, often referred to as a parliament. It scrutinises the government's decisions and holds the government to account. In Wales, the legislature is the Welsh Parliament.

Lobby: an attempt to get a politician or government to do something.

Llywydd: The Llywydd (Presiding Officer) is elected by all Members of the Senedd and serves the Senedd impartially. The Llywydd's main role is to chair Plenary, maintain order and ensure that Standing Orders are followed.

Manifesto: This is a list of promises made by a political party, usually before an election. The manifesto suggests the things that a party will do if they are elected.

Marginal seats: Seats where only a few votes stand between the candidates of the competing parties.

Member Debates: Time is made available by the Business Committee for motions to be proposed by any Member who is not a member of the Government. Member Debates have to be supported by at least two other Members, one of which must represent a different political party. The Business Committee will select a motion for debate from among those tabled.

Minister: Members of government in charge of a specific government department.

Nationalism: The desire for political independence of people who feel they are historically, linguistically or culturally a separate group within a country or geographical area.

Opposition: This term refers to the Members who are not part of the party (or parties) who form the Government. The Opposition will scrutinise the Government.

Parties: These are groups of people who have similar views. Most politicians belong to a political party, although it is possible to be elected as an independent candidate.

Plenary: This is the term used to describe the full meeting of all 60 Members in the Siambr (the main chamber of the Senedd building) to conduct business. Plenary meetings currently take place on Tuesday and Wednesday afternoons during Term Time.

Policies: These are the plans of a political party, usually set out in their manifesto, stating what that party would hope to do if they won the election.

Presiding Officer: See *Llywydd*.

Referendum: The process by which a question is referred to the electorate, who vote on it in a similar way to an election. The Senedd was set up following a 'yes' vote in a referendum held in September 1997.

Regions: For the purposes of the Senedd elections, Wales is divided into five regions: South Wales East; South Wales Central; South Wales West; Mid and West Wales; North Wales. Each region elects four Members using a system of proportional representation, called the Additional Member System.

Representative: A person chosen or elected by one or more people to make choices or act for them.

Republic: A country with an elected head of state, as opposed to a monarch, usually called a president.

Scrutiny: When the Senedd examines the work of the Welsh Government, this process is called 'scrutiny'. This means holding the Welsh Government to account for its decisions and its actions. This job is done by the committees.

Senedd Cymru: The Senedd (or Welsh Parliament) is made up of 60 Members from across Wales. They are elected by the people of Wales to represent them and their communities, make laws for Wales, agree Welsh taxes and to ensure the Welsh Government is doing its job properly.

Short Debate: A Short Debate on a topic proposed by a Member (excluding Members who are also Cabinet Secretaries or Welsh Ministers) is held each week that the Senedd meets in Plenary. They are usually held during the final 30 minutes of the Senedd's Wednesday Plenary meeting.

Selection on Merit: a system employed by the Conservative Party that gives equal opportunity of selection to candidates based on merit and not gender.

Single transferrable vote (STV): a single vote using a system where, if the preferred candidate does not get enough votes to stay in the election, a constituent's vote can be given to their second choice of candidate.

SPAD: Special advisor to a politician.

Stand for election: To join a list of electoral candidates and campaign for votes.

The Senedd: The public building in Cardiff Bay where the business of the Senedd is conducted. The people of Wales have free access to the Senedd and the public gallery, where they can observe the Members in action.

Top of the List: System employed by Plaid Cymru to place women at the top of their party's list of regional top-up candidates in an attempt to enhance the chances of women being elected.

Twinning: A system employed by the Labour Party where two adjacent constituencies would pick a woman in one constituency and a man in the other as a way of balancing selection.

Tŷ Hywel: The main office building housing Senedd staff, meeting rooms, Committee Rooms 4 & 5 and Siambr Hywel (the former debating chamber which is now used as part of the Senedd's education suite).

Vote: A vote in Plenary is generally taken using an electronic voting system. Members may also vote in Plenary or committees by a simple show of hands or a formal role call if required.

Whip: A person who is responsible for maintaining their party's discipline.

Women's rights: Rights for women that are equal to those of men, including equal pay.

Youth Parliament: 60 young people aged between eleven and eighteen who have been elected to represent young people in Wales.

Zipping: A system considered by the Liberal Democrat party where selection would be man – woman; man – woman, etc, to balance gender representation.

About Honno

Honno Welsh Women's Press was set up in 1986 by a group of women who felt strongly that women in Wales needed wider opportunities to see their writing in print and to become involved in the publishing process. Our aim is to develop the writing talents of women in Wales, give them new and exciting opportunities to see their work published and often to give them their first 'break' as a writer. Honno is registered as a community co-operative. Any profit that Honno makes is invested in the publishing programme. Women from Wales and around the world have expressed their support for Honno. Each supporter has a vote at the Annual General Meeting.

Honno, D41,
Hugh Owen Building,
Aberystwyth University,
Aberystwyth, SY23 3DY

Honno Friends
We are very grateful for the support of all our Honno Friends.